Reverend William F. KREKELBERG

SAN JUAN CAPISTRANO MISSION

To Bishop Tod,
This remembrance of the Old Mission
comes with gratitude and a
prayer for your leadership in
the continuing mission.
Bill Krekelberg

Éditions du Signe

In loving memory of
Thomas J. Tracy
From his family:
Erma Jean,
Cynthia and Christina,
Kathryn and Greg,
Kilian and Thomas, Jr.,
And the grandchildren:
Gregory, Remington, and Shane.

Table of Contents

I Beginnings

"Hear the word of the Lord, O nations, proclaim it on distant coasts."
(Jeremiah, 31: 10)

The Setting

When the time came to establish Mission San Juan Capistrano, it wasn't actually the time yet – but no one realized it. Spain's effort to claim and tame Alta California was just six years old. The territory was still a raw frontier, much of it unexplored. There were just two presidios (military outposts) – one at Monterey and the other at San Diego. Five very small missions were just beginning to proclaim a Christian presence in the vast pagan wilderness. All of them were struggling to gain stability. None of them could as yet be called successful.

Mission San Luis Obispo (1772) in the Valley of the Bears was just three years old. Mission San Gabriel (1771), Capistrano's nearest neighbor to the north, was four years old, and so was San Antonio de Padua (1771) in the Sierra de Santa Lucia. Mission San Carlos (1770) in the Carmel Valley near Monterey Bay was five years old. And Mission San Diego (1769), the first and oldest of the missions, although six years old, was still the least successful. There were modest gains at all of them, but there was so much more that needed to be done.

Conditions

The Spanish presence in California consisted primarily of soldiers and missionaries – and not very many of them. In the early years there were no Caucasian women. The Indians wondered how these strange newcomers had come into existence without women. They were already amazed to see animals they had never seen before: cattle, horses, and mules. They speculated that perhaps these alien men were the sons of the she-mules. That mystery would not be solved until later on when colonists, including women and children, arrived to take up residence in the new land.

España

At this time the presidios and missions were far from what we might imagine as the romantic establishments of Old California. There were no glittering whitewashed adobes with red tiled roofs and arched corridors. The reality consisted of protective stockades and very crude structures with flat roofs covered with earth or tules. There were some adobes, but most of the buildings were of palisades, poles set in the ground side by side and plastered inside and out with mud. These crude protective shelters were the best they could do at the time. Life was lived mostly outdoors and that life was definitely not for the fastidious.

When the Franciscans took their vow of poverty, they could hardly have imagined what that would mean for them as missionaries in California. The provisions they brought with them ran out all too soon. They depended heavily on the supply ships sent up annually from San Blas on the Mexican coast. When these delayed or failed, there were hard months of near starvation. Often enough they lived at the mercy and charity of the very Indians they had come to convert and "civilize."

Spanish authorities intended the missions to eventually become self-sustaining, but that time had not yet come and was hardly even foreseeable. Their livestock herds were still small and their agricultural efforts were modest at best. Basic clothing, tools, and other important supplies all had to be imported. The civilized world was far away and the journey by land and sea was long and arduous.

The missionaries did not expect the Indians to easily embrace Christianity. They knew that the early years would be the most difficult. Persuading them to understand and accept Christianity would take time and patience. Baptisms were few in number because, except in danger of death, everyone had to be properly instructed and express their willingness to become a Christian. Then, as now, no one could be validly baptized against his or her own will and without instruction. The neophytes (new Christians) had to understand that after baptism they would be expected to practice a very different way of life.

One of the first problems was communication. Christian Indians had been brought along from Baja to act as interpreters. Often enough, that didn't work because these Indians didn't understand the local language. There were many different dialects and idioms in the mission territory. The missionaries would have to try to learn the native language while the Indians tried to learn some Spanish. Experience taught them that children would learn the fastest and, as they did, they would be able to help the missionaries communicate with the adults.

As is the case generally, the older Indians were more set in their ways and were less likely to grasp and accept Christian ideas. Conversion efforts toward the younger generation were usually more successful. But that, of course, took time. After six years, the missionaries were just beginning to see their hard work and patience produce promising results.

Initially, many of the Indians were afraid of the Spaniards. They seemed like creatures from another world and, in many respects, they were. Their appearance, their dress, the horses they rode, the pack mules, and the cattle absolutely astounded them. The ships in the harbor seemed huge and amazing; unlike any vessel they had ever seen. The booming of a cannon, the smoke and crack of a musket, the clanging of a bell would send them fleeing into the forest and the hills. What were these strangers? Were they men or gods? Were they a blessing or a curse? In the end, curiosity won out over fear. The braver Indians approached and began an encounter that would change their world forever.

Melissa Latham-Stevens

Fascination with the Spaniards and the marvels they possessed increasingly attracted the Indians. The missionaries used this opportunity to further gain their confidence by acts of kindness and gifts of beads and other trinkets. Establishing friendship would be the foundation of religious evangelization.

The Indians were generally affable and welcoming. This did not mean that they couldn't be dangerous. Once the feeling of awe and novelty wore off, the realization that Spaniards were not only human, but also vulnerable became apparent. The Spaniards were hopelessly outnumbered. There were at least 100,000 Indians in California at this time. Any act appearing unkind or threatening could bring a violent response. Bows, arrows, and primitive clubs – though a poor match against powder and ball – could be put to deadly effect. During these first six years such incidents had already happened. Missionary outreach had to be balanced with military vigilance.

Although the soldiers were a necessary component of the Spanish occupation, they could also be a serious problem. The common soldier was a pretty rough character. Far from home – sometimes for years – sexual temptation got the better of them and brought out the worse in them. Assaults against the Indians, women and men, fueled outrage and revenge. They also spread venereal disease, resulting in much suffering and death. The missionaries were angered that such conduct would make enemies of the very people they were trying to befriend and convert. Although generally religious, some soldiers did not share with the Franciscans a strong commitment to Christian morality.

Personalities

Although the pairing of the missionary and the soldier, the "Cross and the Sword," seemed like an ideal approach to win "pagans" over to God and King, the two-headed authority structure resulted in tension and conflict throughout the mission period. Difficulties developed between the principal leaders of both sides early on. Pedro Fages was the Military Commander. Father Junipero Serra was the President of the missions. Fages was responsible for security – the defense and protection of the Spanish presence. Father Serra was responsible for the spread of Christianity among the Indians. Problems seemed inherent and inevitable in these differing purposes. The Commandante needed to be cautious, making sure he had enough men and provisions for protection and defense. The Presidente felt compelled to move on, expand the missions, and establish new ones. The Presidente felt the Commandante was exasperatingly cautious. And the Commandante thought the Presidente was overly and foolishly ambitious.

The Commandante considered his authority superior in Alta California, extending over both soldiers and missionaries. Father Serra considered young Fages as something of a petty martinet who exceeded his authority, constantly finding objections to frustrate missionary efforts. Perhaps, there was also something of a personality clash between the two. The young Commandante wanted to prove himself a prudent military leader. The Father Presidente wanted to prove himself a zealous missionary.

Disgusted with the situation, Serra determined to go back to Mexico and straighten things out with the Viceroy. He left for Mexico City late in October of 1772. Fages could not have been happy to see Serra go over his head and complain to his superior. Indeed, as a result of Serra's meetings, Fages would be relieved of command and Serra would return with both the backing of the Viceroy and a new set of regulations clarifying issues of authority and better promoting the missions.

To Mexico and Back

Father Serra was away from California for one year and four months. Traveling by sea and land it took him three and a half months just to get to Mexico City. On the journey he had been quite ill and, at times, he seemed near death. However, with each setback he recovered and somehow found the strength to carry on his mission. In Mexico City he spent seven months working with both his religious superior and the viceroy, Jose Maria Bucareli.

He personally set forth all the issues, vent his frustrations, and won for his missions both interest and generous support.

Serra's return trip to California took six months. He arrived back at San Diego on March 13, 1774. After recuperating some time, he traveled overland visiting each mission along the way and spreading the good news of the viceroy's help. He probably didn't want to arrive back to Monterey too soon. He would have to deal with Fages who had not yet left California. He finally arrived on May 11th.

After an awkward two weeks, Fages handed over his command to his replacement, Captain Fernando Rivera y Moncada who presented him with his orders on May 24th. Fages, much deflated, remained on at Monterey until July 19th when he went overland to San Diego where he sailed for Mexico on August 4, 1774.

› *El camino real*

An Awkward Beginning

Father Serra's renewed enthusiasm and initial sense of victory didn't last very long. In a rather short time, he became disenchanted with the new military commander. He was not the strength and cheerleader Serra had wanted for the California Missions. He proved to be as conservative and hesitant as his predecessor.

Perhaps Fages had warned Rivera about Serra's aggressive (zealous) manner. The two of them had been together in Monterey for nearly two months prior to Fages's departure. They had plenty of time to talk. And Rivera knew that Fages was dismissed because of Serra's complaints. Rivera decided to keep a prudent and respectful distance from Serra's insistent ambitions. He was determined to preserve his own independence and authority. This was not the attitude that Serra had hoped for. Tensions began to grow and, although relations were official and circumspect, they were not inwardly friendly.

Father Fermín de Lasuén

Father Fermín de Lasuén was just twenty-three when he left Spain to become a missionary in the new world. He was still a deacon when he arrived at the San Fernando College in Mexico City. He was ordained a priest there in 1761 and it is probable that Father Serra, who was there at the time, attended his ordination. Like Father Serra, he was assigned to the Indian Missions in the Mexican Sierra Gorda. After serving there for five years, he joined Father Serra in traveling to the missions of Baja California where Father Serra had become Presidente. He would spend all his time alone in the northern mission of San Francisco de Borja. He served there for five difficult years. Father Serra, who had visited him, thought very highly of his ability and character. Nevertheless, Lasuén found the isolation a great trial.

When the Dominicans replaced the Franciscans in Baja in 1773, Fr. Lasuén joined Father Palóu and five others in an overland trip to the Alta Calilfornia Missions, arriving at San Diego on August 30th. Father Palóu, the Mission Presidente in Alta California while Father Serra was still in Mexico, appointed Lasuén as a supernumerary (an extra priest not yet assigned) to help out at San Gabriel. That mission, like the other missions at that time, was suffering severe hunger because of lack of supplies. He was there when the first Anza Expedition arrived overland from Sonora on March 22, 1774. He was also present when Father Serra stopped there on April 12th, bringing the welcome news of fresh, abundant supplies and the viceroy's wholehearted support.

Fr. Fermin Fran.co de Lasuen

A Controversial Chaplaincy

During Rivera's duty in Lower California he had become a close friend of Father Lasuén. Rivera was the Captain and Military Commander at Loreto and Lasuén was the missionary at San Francisco de Borja. When Rivera came up to take over as Military Commander of Alta California, he was pleased to find his friend serving at San Gabriel. He invited him to become his personal advisor and chaplain at the Monterey Presidio. This appealed to Lasuén who did not like San Gabriel ("It is a place most repugnant to me."). Besides, he was frustrated that he had been in the Upper California missions for two years and had not yet been assigned a mission of his own. In fact he had asked permission to return to the Missionary College in Mexico City. Now this opportunity to be the comandante's chaplain seemed to be the only bright spot in an otherwise depressing situation. He was flattered and liked the idea very much, but he knew that such an assignment would have to come from his superior, Father Serra.

When Lasuén enthusiastically wrote to Serra asking for the Rivera chaplaincy, it was not met with an enthusiastic response. Thinking he would have better results in person, Father Lasuén impetuously joined a pack train headed for Monterey. He received a cold reception from Father Serra at Carmel who felt that the requested chaplaincy would be an alliance of one of his own with someone he did not like. Serra was not inclined to do anything to please Rivera. Why should he favor someone who was proving to be so unfavorable to him? Nevertheless, Father Serra, after careful thought, set aside his personal feelings and reluctantly allowed Lasuén to take the assignment.

Lasuén moved to Monterey and took up duties there on July 4th. Rather naively, he asked Serra if Father Gregorio Amurrió could join him as an assistant and companion. Serra, who thought that even one in that assignment was too many, declined the request. Furthermore, it wasn't an assignment that was destined to last very long.

Confrontation

A major confrontation between Father Serra and Captain Rivera was about to take place. As usual, Serra was anxious to establish more missions. Late in May, both he and Rivera had received a letter from Viceroy Bucareli calling for the establishment of missions in the San Francisco Bay area. The second Anza Expedition with soldiers and colonists was on its way for that purpose. Bucareli also directed that other missions selected by Father Serra should be established without delay.

Serra's copy of the letter was in Bucareli's difficult handwriting. Rivera's copy was in the clear hand of a secretary. Serra had erroneously read that each mission was to have a guard of thirteen of Anza's soldiers. Rivera's copy clearly showed that it should be six. Almost childishly, Rivera allowed Serra to persist in his misunderstanding until such a time as he might embarrass him in his error.

On August 10, Serra received another letter from Bucareli authorizing the long postponed Channel Missions. Because of the numerous Indians there, each mission would have to have an extra heavy guard. In a meeting at the presidio of August 12, Rivera made it clear to Serra that only one mission could be provided with a sufficient guard and that would have to be just six soldiers. Serra objected. In his mind it was thirteen. The argument became quite angry and heated. When Rivera dramatically produced his copy of Bucareli's letter clearly showing the number to be six, Serra was taken aback and embarrassed at his mistake. Rivera was quite incensed that his integrity was challenged and made known his sense of outrage. He was 50 years old and had spent 33 years in the military. And, although Serra was his senior at 62, he did not appreciate a civilian, especially a religious, questioning his judgment and authority.

San Juan Capistrano

1775

After a night's sleep and a prayerful Sunday Mass, they met again the next day, August 13th, and tried to address the issues more calmly. They agreed the Bay area missions would have to await the arrival of the Anza Expedition. They also agreed that San Buenaventura on the Channel would have to be postponed. That populous area required more soldiers. By way of compromise they agreed to establish a mission between San Diego and San Gabriel – Mission San Juan Capistrano. This mission would require less soldiers and had easy access to the San Diego Presidio should any trouble arise. It wasn't what either of them had planned, but it was what Providence directed.

Now it was a matter of settling the details. Father Serra asked Captain Rivera for the temporary loan of a few extra soldiers to the help the mission get started. In this new day of cooperation, this was not a problem.

The Capistrano compromise presented Serra with an ironic opportunity. Father Lasuén had complained about not having a mission of his own. Captain Rivera had pressured Serra to appoint Lasuén as his presidio chaplain. Father Serra now declared that he should leave his recent chaplaincy and become the founding missionary of San Juan Capistrano. Lasuén was present when Serra and Rivera agreed on Capistrano. Serra turned to him and said, "Well, Father Lasuén, now Your Reverence has a mission; had it been San Buenaventura, it would be yours, but this is one that he (Rivera) is in a position to found."

Rivera did not like this surprise turn of events and neither did Lasuén who wrote a few days later to a confidant: "It is a place for which precisely I have always had little inclination." Nevertheless, in the spirit of the good missionary that he was, he proceeded to his assignment with holy obedience and resignation. Father Serra and Captain Rivera decided that in the interest of peace they would communicate with each other in writing. Thus it was that Mission San Juan Capistrano came about because of, and in spite of, these good men.

Father Gregorio Amurrió

Father Lasuén was not to be alone in this endeavor. Father Serra had paired him up with Father Gregorio Amurrió. Both were from the same Spanish province, Cantabria. Both had become Franciscans at the Convento de San Francisco in Vitoria. Both had also served in the Lower California Missions. And when the Dominicans had taken over those missions, they had traveled overland together to San Diego and the missions of Upper California. Father Lasuén was the older of the two by eight years. In 1775 he was 39 and Amurrió was 31.

Father Amurrió had served at San Diego as a supernumerary until Father Serra arrived back from Mexico in 1774. Serra appointed him as chaplain to the ship "Santiago" when it departed San Diego for Monterey. From there he proceeded to San Luis Obispo where he was spared all the unhappy negotiations that occurred in Monterey and Carmel. He served at San Luis Obispo until his appointment to San Juan Capistrano in the summer of 1775.

Title and Patron

The title and patron, San Juan Capistrano (1385 – 1456), was the next one on the list decided by the viceroy. He was, of course, a Franciscan saint whose name, perhaps, had been suggested by Father Serra. The viceroy who authorized and supported the missions had the honor of naming them.

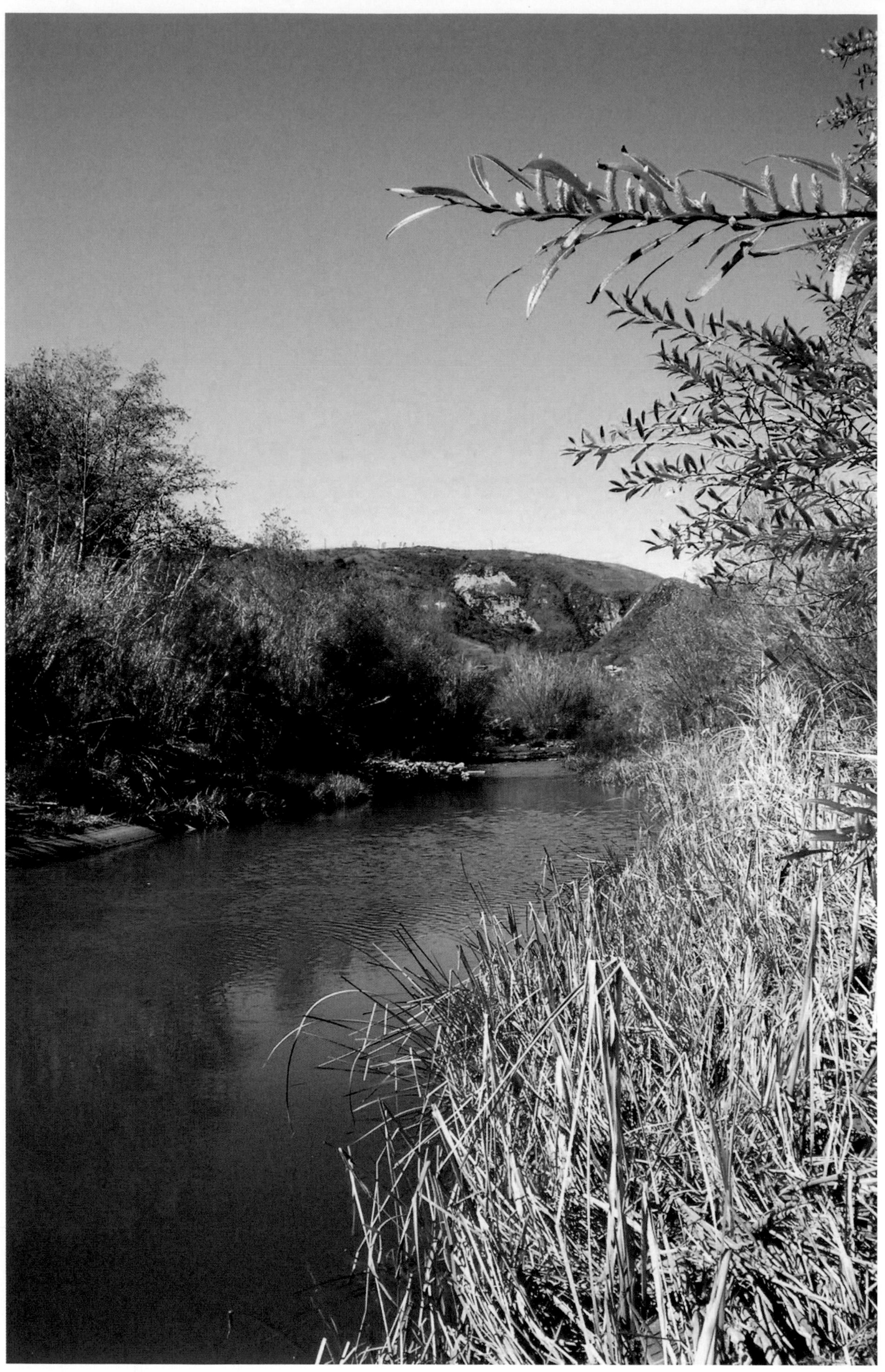

The mission's water sources: ❯ *Trabuco creek*

San Juan creek

Founding San Juan Capistrano

The Founding Document

As President of the California Missions Father Serra wrote this document formally establishing Mission San Juan Capistrano, appointing its missionaries, and designating its initial supplies:

"Viva Jesus, Maria, Joseph

"The Mission of San Juan Capistrano which is about to be established in the valley of the same name or in its vicinity between the Missions of San Diego and San Gabriel of the Earthquakes, about twenty leagues from both and two from the coastline of the South Sea, according to the agreement made between the Captain, Comandante Don Fernando de Rivera y Moncada and the Father President of the Missions, Father Junípero Serra, on the thirteenth day of August 1775 by order and instructions of His Excellency the Viceroy of this New Spain, sent on the 24th of May and received on the first of August of the same year.

"Arrangements

"I assigned and named as Ministers and Missionaries for this new Mission:

Father Preacher Fray Fermín Francisco de Lasuén and Father Preacher Fray Gregorio Amurrió.

"For the escort the Comandante accepted only two of the four soldiers offered by the Missions, and he added four from the Presidios. These were: six soldiers (leather jackets) and a muleteer named Feliciano.

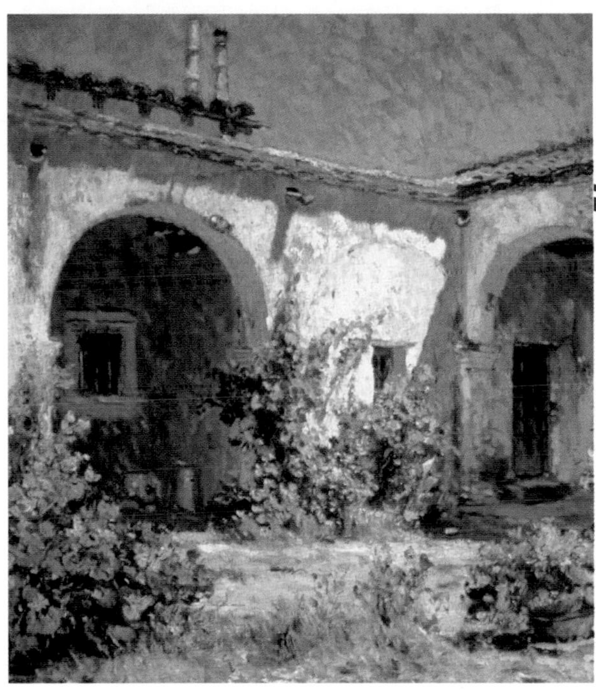

Colin Campbell Cooper. Irvine Museum

"Of the Indians assigned to assist our Religious with their labors in the founding of this Mission, who came with the authority of His Excellency the Viceroy and of their own free will, and who left Baja California with the departure of our missionaries: two Families of man and wife and four Indian boys unmarried.

"Regarding provisions, the Comandante, in accordance with my petition, granted:

Four tercios of fine flour, two others of unsifted flour, three tercios of beans, one tercio of rice and an order on the granary of San Diego for twenty-five fanegas of corn.

"And to please the natives (gentiles) and reciprocate their gifts, I gave to Father Lasuén four strings of beads of different colors.

"Concerning the cattle and cows that have just arrived at San Diego from Baja California, I assigned to this Mission: nine milch (chichiguas) cows and a breed bull and a yoke of oxen from San Buenaventura and moreover I shall take care of their replacement when the desired foundation is realized.

"Regarding mules and horses, the Fathers of this Mission have been assigned and have received: eight pack mules, six broken and two unbroken and three saddle mules, three horses broken and two mares, one of these with its colt.

"Regarding pigs, the Mission San Diego will give a male and female; regarding chickens, it or San Gabriel will give what they can. The same will give two saddles with their trappings and bridles for the Fathers and two others also furnished for vaqueros.

"Regarding tools, I gave Father Lasuen: twelve new, large hoes, two axes for clearing or preparing charcoal, six large machetes for cleaning up (brush,etc.), six new knives, and the branding iron with this mark 'CAP'.

"For plowshares I have written to the Fathers of San Gabriel that while awaiting their supplies from Mexico they should satisfy their needs from the stores of San Buenaventura, which are kept at that Mission, for pickaxes, plowshares, and other iron tools.

"They have for the Church and Sacristy: a crucifix for the altar; one canvas portrait of more than a vara in length of the Virgin Mary, Domina Pastora, which has a condemned man on her shoulders, which Father Campa used; another canvas portrait, a little more than a third of a vara, of Our Lady of Soledad; among others a portrait of the Holy Patron (San Juan Capistrano); about four varas of muslin to make a baldachino and backdrop for the altar; a new Missal with the Saints of our Order; a number of double corporals of fine linen with burse and pall; an Amice of Breton lace, and two purificators of fine linen; a rochet of Bramant linen, with floral design and lace; and Castile Wax for Masses for a year. The wine will be furnished from the nearby missions as their supply allows.

"To this Mission have been allotted all of the ornaments of those that have come from Baja California for the Church as well as the house; also within those ornaments will be found those for the use of the other two Ministers, and the two Fathers, (Juan) Prestamero and Imas.

"For the celebration of Mass, the Mission of San Diego will give a chalice, which up to the present day has had no other use but to serve travelers; and from the Mission of San Buenaventura, the Fathers of San Gabriel will give a vestment of various colors. In the meantime also from there, the oils, surplice, Ritual, Baptismal shell and all the other requisites and a bell.

"The Mission of San Antonio has given two blank books bound in red leather for entries.

"With these beginnings and arrangements, Father Fermín left this Mission of San Carlos de Monterey on the 21st of August 1775 in order to join with his

Religious companion in the Mission of San Luis Obispo. May God bless them. Amen.

Father Junípero Serra"

Alexander F. Harmer c. 1875. Irvine Museum

Preparations

On Tuesday, August 15, the Celebration of the Assumption of Mary, Father Lasuén announced to his presidio congregation that he had been assigned to found the Capistrano mission. That afternoon six ladies and three girls went over to Carmel to protest the transfer and plead with Father Serra to allow him to stay. However moved he may have been, the Father President held to his decision.

On Thursday of that week, Father Serra wrote Viceroy Bucareli informing him of the decision to found Mission Capistrano and he included a copy of the founding document. On the same day, Father Lasuén wrote Father Francisco Pangua, the Guardian at the San Fernando College in Mexico City, expressing his acceptance of the assignment and asking for his prayers: "I humbly beg your pious blessing for the happy outcome of the task so recently entrusted to me. I have already made a beginning, for I have taken steps to obtain the implements we shall need."

On Sunday, August 20th, Father Serra met with Captain Rivera in a personal, heart to heart conversation hoping to clean the air and restore harmony. Rivera, still feeling wounded, listened to Serra's overtures but did not accept them. Though officially courteous, he was not "ready to make nice."

"We shall undertake the journey and the task assigned to us. May God be with us to be our helper. Amen"
(Lasuen, August 17, 1775)

On Monday, August 21, just eight days after his appointment, Father Lasuén left Monterey with an Indian servant and an escort of nine soldiers. They traveled to San Luis Obispo where they picked up Father Gregorio Amurrió and made their way to San Gabriel. Here they left Father Amurrió behind in charge of organizing the necessary supplies. Then they continued on to San Diego where Father Lasuén met with Lieutenant José Francisco Ortega, the Presidio Commander. They made plans to reconnoiter a suitable site for the new mission.

It is known from Father Lasuen's letters that he kept a diary to record the details of this project.

Unfortunately, that diary has gone missing and so we know very little about the daily happenings over the next ten weeks.

We do know that sometime during that period that Father Lasuén and Lieutenant Ortega – presumably with an escort of soldiers – went up from San Diego to an area nearly midway between it and San Gabriel. They chose a site near a stream called La Quema (the burn). This name had come into use because all who traveled through it remembered that there had been a significant grass fire there. That stream is now called San Juan Creek.

Father Lasuén reported to his superior in Mexico: "We have experienced all the labor that goes with the selection of a site for a mission and all the happiness that can come where a foundation is made in a good location. And ours was a good location near the stream La Quema and three-quarters of a league from the Camino Real in the direction of the coast."

Following their return to San Diego some of the soldiers balked at the task of assisting in the founding of the new mission. On October 6, Father Lasuen thought that perhaps he and Father Amurrió might have unwittingly said or did something that offended the soldiers. He expressed his concern to Lt. Ortega: "I wish to know if they have some grievance against the two of us, and if so, if they will speak to us about it."

The soldiers objected to the meager rations they would get while helping to found the new mission. They thought they might be better off at the presidio, even though the supplies there were rather poor. Indeed, Lasuén himself would later write that, "When I left Monterey for my mission, the majority of the missionaries told me they would not undertake such a project with such inadequate supplies and equipment."

They also objected to the physical work of putting up the buildings on that site. They argued that they weren't paid to do that kind of work. They were soldiers and not common laborers. Besides, as it turned out, one of them had harbored a grudge against Father Lasuén who had reprimanded him for claiming a mule that actually belonged to the new mission. Father Lasuén was surprised to hear this because he thought he had been gentle in insisting on the mission's right.

Elizabeth Borglum c. 1895. Irvine Museum

Ortega was upset with his soldiers' attitude and with the obvious challenge to his own authority. He told them that he himself intended to work along side the padre in preparing the shelters. Rather dramatically, he drew his sword and questioned their loyalty: "Am I commanding here loyal servants of the King or traitors? Are you servants of His Majesty?" (Father Lasuén would later recall that the rebellious soldiers were actually confronted at gunpoint.) Seeing that their Comandante had run out of patience, they said they would, of course, carry out his orders. Ortega chose the ones he considered the most dependable.

First Founding 1775

On Thursday, October 19, Father Lasuen, Lieutenant Ortega, a sergeant, and twelve soldiers set out from San Diego to the site of the new mission. It took them nine days to cover the distance. They were still on the road on the feast day of San Juan Capistrano, October 23rd. They arrived at the mission site on Sunday, October 29th. About this time a messenger was sent ahead to Father Amurrió at San Gabriel telling him to come down with the cattle and supplies. The next day became the official day of foundation, October 30th. They performed the customary ritual of taking possession of the lands for the King. A large cross was prepared, blessed, raised, and venerated. Father Lasuén celebrated the first Mass in a simple enrcmada or shelter.

Construction

During the next eight days preliminary work began preparing the site for its first crude buildings. The curious Indians attracted to these activities seemed welcoming and friendly. They eagerly joined in the work along with the padre and the less than eager soldiers. They prepared a corral for the animals; staked out an outline for the church and dwelling; dug holes for the poles that make up the buildings. They also cut and hauled timber to the site along with the tule that would be used for the roofs.

Disaster at San Diego

After that first week everything changed drastically. On Tuesday, November 7th, at about three o'clock in the afternoon, Joseph Maíia Verdugo, a courier from San Diego rode in with the shocking news that Mission San Diego had been attacked and burned and that Father Luís Jayme and two others had been killed.

Ortega must have been stunned. This was his jurisdiction. He was in command – and he was away from his post. Who knew what might happen next? Furthermore, the Indians who had been helping at Capistrano had disappeared. Perhaps they too were now aware of what had happened and might now be preparing their own attack. The mission site was too exposed. He and Lasuén agreed that it would have to be abandoned and they needed to get back to the presidio as soon as possible.

Later that same day, in the evening, Father Amurrió and a soldier escort showed up with the cattle and supplies, after a nearly fifty-mile journey. It would be a short stay and a dangerous one. In fact, Father Amurrió's first day together with Father Lasuén at Capistrano would also be their last.

Ortega stayed as long as he had to. He waited until everyone was organized and prepared, but he couldn't accompany the slower moving pack train. He left the missionaries with nine soldiers, instructing them to stay together and be as vigilant as possible. He left at six o'clock in the evening on the next day, riding through the night and arriving at the presidio at eleven o'clock the next morning. The padres, their escort, and the cattle and supplies arrived two days later at nightfall. Everyone was relieved, but worried about what might happen next. The joy of establishing a new mission had turned into fear and a profound sorrow.

The days that followed were an unsettling mixture of sadness and fear. Indian shouts were heard in the night. Still reeling from the first disaster, no one knew if the Indians might regroup and try to finish them off. This time the presidio soldiers would not be caught off guard. They were alert and ready to defend themselves.

Lieutenant Ortega began a preliminary inquiry. Who organized the attack? Why was it that the presidio was unaware of the attack on the mission? He knew as commander he would be held responsible. He interviewed Mission Indians who had remained faithful and conducted forays into the countryside and villages to round up suspects.

Monterey

It took over a month for the news to reach Monterey headquarters. Couriers arrived at the presidio on December 13th. Captain Rivera immediately went over to Carmel and informed Father Serra. It was an almost "I-told-you-so!" atmosphere. Rivera had staunchly resisted Serra's zeal in promoting new missions. He had always argued that there were not enough soldier guards. Now his fears had been realized at Mission San Diego. Rebellious Indians had taken advantage of the fact that guards had been drawn away from both San Diego's mission and presidio. Rivera's unspoken recrimination was not lost on the Father Presidente. Later, in a letter to Father Pangua at the San Fernando Mission College in Mexico, he would confide that, "I am very much inclined to think that they may wish to blame the loss of Mission San Diego on the founding of San Juan Capistrano and the impertinent zeal of the religious to found new missions." Nevertheless, he wasn't about to cower before that insinuation: "I am quite sure there is no foundation whatever for such an accusation."

Captain Rivera prepared to leave Monterey with troops to reinforce San Diego and punish the attackers. Father Serra was also anxious to go down and assess the situation for himself. Rivera objected saying he would be traveling very fast and could not be slowed down. Serra had a chronic problem with his leg; he asked if he could follow with a separate soldier escort. The answer was "No." Rivera claimed he could not spare the troops. It was clear that the Comandante Militar did not want Father Serra with him in San Diego.

Plea for Mercy

Serra's actions would have to be confined to his prayers and his pen. He immediately wrote Viceroy Bucareli and – it is amazing considering the situation – he pleaded for mercy and pardon for the Indian attackers. Severe punishment would not be a good example of Christian forgiveness and it would only impede missionary work by driving the Indians away. He also asked that both the San Diego and Capistrano Missions be re-established as soon as possible and at their previous locations. A temporary setback, no matter how severe – must not be allowed to be a permanent defeat. Serra could only wait and pray. It would be over six months before he could get transportion to San Diego.

Meanwhile, Rivera didn't travel quite as fast as he had told Serra he would. It took him nearly three weeks to get to San Gabriel. There he met up with Lieutenant Colonel Juan Bautista de Anza and his party of soldiers and colonists who were headed for the proposed establishment at San Francisco Bay. Anza, on hearing of the situation at San Diego, volunteered to help Captain Rivera. On January 7, both left for San Diego: Anza with seventeen of his soldiers and Rivera with his ten. They arrived on January 11th, nearly a month since Rivera had left Monterey.

Inquiry at San Diego

Captain Rivera began his official investigation of the San Diego disaster. Besides the Indians already in custody and those yet to be rounded up, he put the blame squarely on the shoulders of Lieutenant Ortega, the presidio commander. He should have been at his post and not so accommodating to the missionaries founding Capistrano. Amazingly, Rivera excused the sentry on duty the night of the attack, even though it was obvious to everyone that he should have been aware of what was going on and sounded the alarm.

After three weeks, it was apparent to Anza that no campaign would be launched against the Indians. Seeing there was no longer a crisis at San Diego, he decided to get on with his original orders and leave with his troops for the north.

Carlos

One of the principal suspects in the attack, a Mission Indian named Carlos, had eluded capture. Rather than being caught and, perhaps, killed in a fight, he sneaked into the presidio one night and claimed sanctuary in the building then being used as a church. In spite of objections from the padres, Rivera and some of this men violated sanctuary by forcibly removing Carlos and imprisoning him. On March 8th, Father Vicente Fuster in accord with the Capistrano missionaries, Fathers Lasuén and Amurrió, declared the Military Commander excommunicated under Church law. (Naturally, this put a major strain on the now disintegrating friendship between the Captain and his former chaplain, Lasuén.) After a few very uncomfortable days, Rivera left San Diego to consult with the Father Presidente at Carmel. He arrived there on April 15th. Father Serra advised him that the excommunication was valid and that for the good of his soul he needed to return to San Diego, seek absolution, and return the prisoner to the sanctuary. On May 18th, he was back at San Diego where he accepted guilt and was absolved. He restored Carlos to the sanctuary and, afterwards, the missionaries brought him out and he was again placed in custody. Rivera had been humiliated before everyone, but, to his credit, he was more concerned about his standing before God.

Serra Arrives

Before long, Father Serra finally found a way to get to San Diego. In May the ship "San Antonio" arrived at Monterey Bay with supplies. Father Serra received permission from its Captain, Diego de Choquet, to sail with him on his way south to San Diego. They left on June 29th and arrived at San Diego in just twelve days.

The missionaries were surprised to see Father Serra on board, but not as surprised as Captain Rivera. The last time Serra had made such a trip he was on his way to Mexico City where he had Fages removed from his command. Although Serra had no such dark intentions, Rivera, suddenly not feeling well at all, took to his quarters.

Serra had come to console and encourage his disheartened missionaries. It had been eight months since the attack on the San Diego Mission. During this time the missionaries had to put up with all the hardships of frontier life without the satisfaction of doing missionary work. They all felt discouraged; their time was being wasted and they might as well return to Mexico and their San Fernando College. Serra knew that if he couldn't get things going again, he would lose them. Using his powers of pursuasion and inciting them with his own zeal, he encouraged them to hang on and continue the course.

Serra pressured Rivera to allow the reconstruction of the San Diego Mission. Captain Choquet of the "San Antonio" volunteered to do the work along with his sailors. On August 8th, seventeen days into the project, Rivera called off the work citing a rumor of another Indian attack. Disgusted, Serra and the work party returned to the presidio. This definitely was not in accord with his motto: "Always look forward, never back!" Frustration and disintegrating morale deepened for nearly two months.

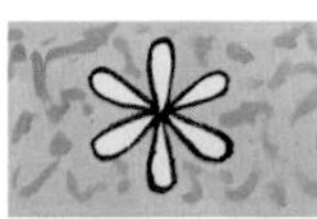

Serra

Gloom to Gladness

Progress was being made even though they didn't know about it. In the north, Lieutenant Joaquín Moraga had established the San Francisco Presidio on July 28th. And in the south, good news was steadily approaching.

In San Diego gloom turned into gladness on September 28th. Couriers brought orders from Viceroy Bucareli: Two missions must be founded at San Francisco Bay; twenty-five soldiers were being sent as reinforcements; the guilty Indian prisoners were to be released at once and treated kindly; and, finally, both Missions of San Diego and San Juan Capistrano were to be established without delay at their previous locations.

Of course, Father Serra was exuberant. The viceroy had backed him up and agreed with his suggestions. In his excitement Serra ordered the bells to be rung in jubilation. The next day, September 29th, the Feast of Saint Michael, he sang a High Mass in thanksgiving and "for the health and happiness of His Excellency." He wrote to the viceroy that the good news he had sent "filled the cup of our joy to overflowing."

Although he was happy to receive the twenty-five reinforcements who arrived on that same day, Captain Rivera did not share the same measure of good cheer. As directed, he ordered the two missions to be re-established. He conferred with Father Serra on how that should be done. He also made his own plans to set out for San Francisco and establish the mission there, which the viceroy in his letters presumed had already happened. In fact, it had been done, although Rivera didn't know about it. He had permitted only the founding of the presidio, but contrary to those wishes, Lt. Colonel Anza ordered Lt. Moraga to help establish the mission anyway. On October 14th, two weeks after receiving the viceroy's letters, Captain Rivera and thirteen soldiers left San Diego.

Father Lasuén went with him. Father Pangua from the Missionary College had sent permission restoring him to Rivera's chaplaincy. He now accompanied him with some hesitancy. He had begun to doubt the Captain's friendship and intentions. Besides, Rivera was ready to quit Alta California. He had written to his military friends in Mexico City that it had been the place of "the greatest tribulation and sorrow he had experienced." He had spoken of retirement and had sent a letter requesting it in August. He didn't know it yet, but orders for his transfer were already on their way.

Following Rivera's departure, Serra got busy re-establishing the two missions. Since Lasuén was no longer available, he sent word to Father Pablo Mugártegui at San Luis Obispo to come down and join Father Amurrió as missionaries for San Juan Capistrano. Father Fuster with some Mission Indians and an escort of twelve soldiers began to restore Mission San Diego. By October 17th a good start had been made and the initial buildings were ready for occupation.

San Juan Capistrano Renewed

On October 25th, Father Junípero Serra set out from San Diego to personally re-found Mission San Juan Capistrano. With him was his servant, a Mission Indian from Baja, and Capistrano's missionary-designate, Father Gregorio Amurrió. Their military escort consisted of Corporal Nicholás Carabanas and ten soldiers: Jacinto Gloria, José Antonio Peña, Francisco Peña, Pio Quinto Zuñiga, Nicholás Gomez, Manuel Robles, Matias Vega, José Dolores Dominguez, Julian Acebedo, and José Joaquin Armenta. Father Serra noted that three of these, lacking horses, were foot soldiers. A pack train carried all their equipment and supplies.

Before he left, Captain Rivera had given strict orders to the soldiers. They were to build their own shelters and to assist the padres in whatever was necessary for the mission. However, he exempted them from the tedious, menial and presumably demeaning work of mixing mortar and making bricks. This, no doubt, was considered Indian work.

They all arrived sometime at the end of the month. The cross, raised the year before, was still in place. They dug up the millstones and the bells. They hung up the bells; built a temporary shelter; and constructed an arbor in which they placed an altar in preparation for Mass and the founding ceremonies.

All Saints Day 1776

On November 1, 1776, the Feast of All Saints, Father Serra blessed the holy water, the site, the cross, and the bells. Afterwards, he sang the Solemn Mass and preached a sermon. The bells were rung to mark the occasion and to announce their presence and this new beginning. The local Indians gathered to welcome them and expressed their pleasure at their return. In this way, the seventh of California's twenty-one missions began its many years of service.

On the same day, Father Serra wrote Bucareli and announced the founding which he knew "would be a source of delight and happiness" for the viceroy. He poured out his own joy and gratitude: "I send Your Excellency my sincerest and heartfelt thanks and congratulations, because, after God, we owe it all to Your Excellency for the well being of many – and most especially of these new establishments – in His holy love and grace."

Serra described San Juan Capistrano as midway between "San Diego Mission and San

Goode

Goode

Gabriel de los Temblores Mission: and on the same spot where, last year, it had been planned and started." He went on to write "This place has plenty of water, pasture, wood, timber, and, in particular, there are many rancherías (villages), and we have been met everywhere with cordiality. To give them instruction will not be very difficult – easier in fact, than has been the case with the other missions founded before this. While their language is not entirely the same as that of San Gabriel, many from there know the language of this place, and vice-versa, as they are neighboring nations, and are in constant touch with each other."

The next day, he wrote his superior Father Pangua in Mexico City. He was so elated about San Juan Capistrano that he suggested a holiday might be declared in its honor at the Missionary College. In this way his missionary friends, far away, might share in the joy of this advance of the Christian gospel in California.

Father Serra called the place San Juan Capistrano de Quanis-savit. He wrote this title on the first page of the mission sacramental books. Later Quanis-savit was crossed out and replaced with Sajirit. This may be because he misunderstood the pronunciation from the Indians, or, perhaps, the name was changed when the mission was relocated in 1778 to another site.

On November 3rd, Father Serra left Capistrano for San Gabriel where he intended to gather the cattle; additional supplies of food and equipment; and some Mission Indians who could help with the construction work, act as interpreters, and, especially, help with teaching religion. Supplies specifically for San Juan Capistrano had not yet arrived from Mexico. To make up for this, Serra took from the supplies stored at San Gabriel for the founding of San Buenaventura. This mission had been continually postponed because of an in sufficient number of soldiers to provide protection in that very populous area. Serra would later reflect that if he had simply named the Capistrano site "San Buenaventura", then there would have been less confusion and paperwork in transferring the goods. Fortunately, it didn't occur to him soon enough. If it had, later generations would be waiting annually for the swallows to return to San Buenaventura.

Provisions

Capistrano was nurtured from several sources. Some provisions came from the royal storehouse at the San Diego Presidio. It also received food donations from Missions San Gabriel and San Luis Obispo. But it received most of its provisions from the goods stored at San Gabriel for San Buenaventura. Besides utensils, dry goods, equipment, and food, it also had eighty-three head of cattle, twelve mules, and a yoke of oxen. The supplies obtained from the royal storehouse included chocolate (almost considered an essential by the padres), wine for Mass, flour, corn, beans, and a few utensils such as a copper stew pot and a frying pan. Curiously, the bells used at Capistrano were the bells of San Gabriel. That mission preferred the bells designated for San Buenaventura. Perhaps this was because of their size, weight, and the difficulty of transportation.

Within a few months Father Serra ordered a painting of the mission's patron, San Juan Capistrano. He was very particular about it, suggesting its size, color (a gray Franciscan habit, not a blue one), and even the Mexican artist – he preferred the work of José de Paez. He asked that it be sent first to his home mission at Monterey because, "It would give me much pleasure to see it." This painting arrived before the summer of 1777 and is hanging in the Mission Basilica.

Danger on the Trail

Serra did not stay long at San Gabriel. As soon as he was able to gather together the livestock, supplies, and a number of Mission Indian helpers, he headed back to Capistrano. Anxious to get there as soon as possible, he went ahead of the slow pack train with the cattle; a soldier, José Antonio Peña; and an Indian interpreter. At a point along the road, about half way down to Capistrano near the Trabuco Creek, they were surprised and confronted by a large crowd of painted and well-armed Indians. Their yelling and menacing behavior filled them with fear. Some had arrows at the bowstrings and were ready to let them fly. Father later recalled that he was sure that he had come to the end of his life. Fortunately the Mission Indian companion saved them. He shouted back at the Indians in their own tongue, telling them that many soldiers would soon be coming up the road and would kill them all if they did any harm. The warriors backed down. Father Serra had the presence of mind to see a spiritual opportunity. He began to bless the Indians individually with a sign of the cross on their foreheads and distributed to them some gifts of glass beads. Afterwards, they proceeded on their way unmolested and grateful for escaping what had seemed like certain death.

On November 12th, Corporal Nicholás Beltrán reported the incident to Lieutenant Ortega at the San Diego Presidio. On November 15th, he sent Sergeant Mariano Carrillo to investigate the situation. Carrillo reported back that all was quiet and peaceable, but that two soldiers and an Indian servant had deserted.

An Assault

The hostility of the Indians on the road seemed a contradiction to the friendly welcome Serra had experienced when he first arrived to re-establish the mission. A likely explanation is revealed in Carrillo's report to Ortega. He stated that two Indian chiefs had come to Capistrano and had asked permission to settle there. One of them, however, complained that a soldier had sexually assaulted his wife. Father Serra, very upset, demanded that this soldier, Manuel Robles, be removed from the Mission guard. Carrillo replaced him with another soldier and took him back to the presidio to face charges.

Franciscan historian, Father Zephyrin Engelhardt has written about this affair: "It does amaze that such a scandal could happen within three weeks of the founding of the Mission, and that the presence of the Father President himself failed to check the criminal propensities of a member of the guard."

Unfortunately, this was not an isolated incident. The following June, Father Serra wrote to Father Pangua: "In San Juan Capistrano it seems that all the sad experiences that we went through at the beginning have come to life again. The soldiers, without any restraint or shame, have behaved like brutes toward the Indian women." Throughout the mission chain and the Mission Period the scandalous conduct of some of the Christian soldiers would prove to be both an upset to the Indians and a serious obstacle to the missionaries who were trying their best to teach Christian morality.

Off to a Better Start

A little over a month later, Father Serra bid farewell to Father Gregorio and began his long journey overland to his home, Mission San Carlos at Carmel. He arrived at San Gabriel on December 6th and, just two hours later, Father Pablo Mugártegui also arrived on his his long journey down from San Luis Obispo. He had with him that mission's donation of food, garbanzos and corn – "as much as the mules could carry."

Father Junípero Serra reflected that Mission San Juan Capistrano was off to a good start, as far as provisions were concerned. He was confidant that they currently "lacked for nothing" and that greater supplies were expected from Mexico. When he left Capistrano the basic structures were well underway. The padres' house had been built, complete with a door and its lock. A corral was in place for the livestock and the church building was already taking shape. But most of all, he thought highly of the two missionaries, Fathers Mugártegui and Amurrió, and was confident that they would do good work. He wrote the viceroy, "The zeal, talents and religious spirit of both of them give grounds for every hope that their labors will be blessed with speedy and pronounced success." Later on, Serra would write that the new governor, Felipe de Neve, had been very impressed with them when he passed through Capistrano on his way north to Monterey: "The Governor was much edified at seeing the cheerfulness of the missionaries in the midst of their poverty. For the Fathers down there, and their mission, he had a warm spot in his heart, and is very anxious to do something for them."

A Christian Mission

Of course, San Juan Capistrano was a Christian Mission and hoped to incorporate the Indian inhabitants into Christ's Word and Spirit. Father Serra's long time friend, Father Francisco Palóu wrote about Father Serra and San Juan Capistrano in his book, "Vida," the first biography of Junipero Serra:

"With the aid of the interpreter whom the Venerable Father President and Founder brought along from San Gabriel, he lost no time in telling the pagans the principal purpose which induced the fathers to come thither and live among them was to teach them the way to heaven, to make them Christian, so they would save their souls, etc. They understood this so rapidly, and they were so impressed by the statement, that they soon began to ask for baptism. The result was that (as the priests wrote at the beginning), just as the pagans of other missions had been a nuisance in asking the fathers for food and other small gifts, those of San Juan Capistrano were a nuisance in asking for baptism, thus making the period of instruction seem very long to them. By this earnestness and through the aid rendered, the spiritual work was given impetus. In a short time, the first baptisms were administered. The number of baptisms increased to such an extent that when the Venerable Father Fray Junípero died, the mission had 472 natives from that place and neighboring villages. A short time after his edifying death, the number began to increase still more."

Carlos III
King of Spain

Alta California
1776
San Francisco
San Carlos
San Antonio de Padua
San Luis Obispo
San Gabriel
San Juan Capistrano
San Diego

·PLAN·
·OF·
·MISSION·SAN·JUAN·CAPISTRANO

·SCALE ·FT·

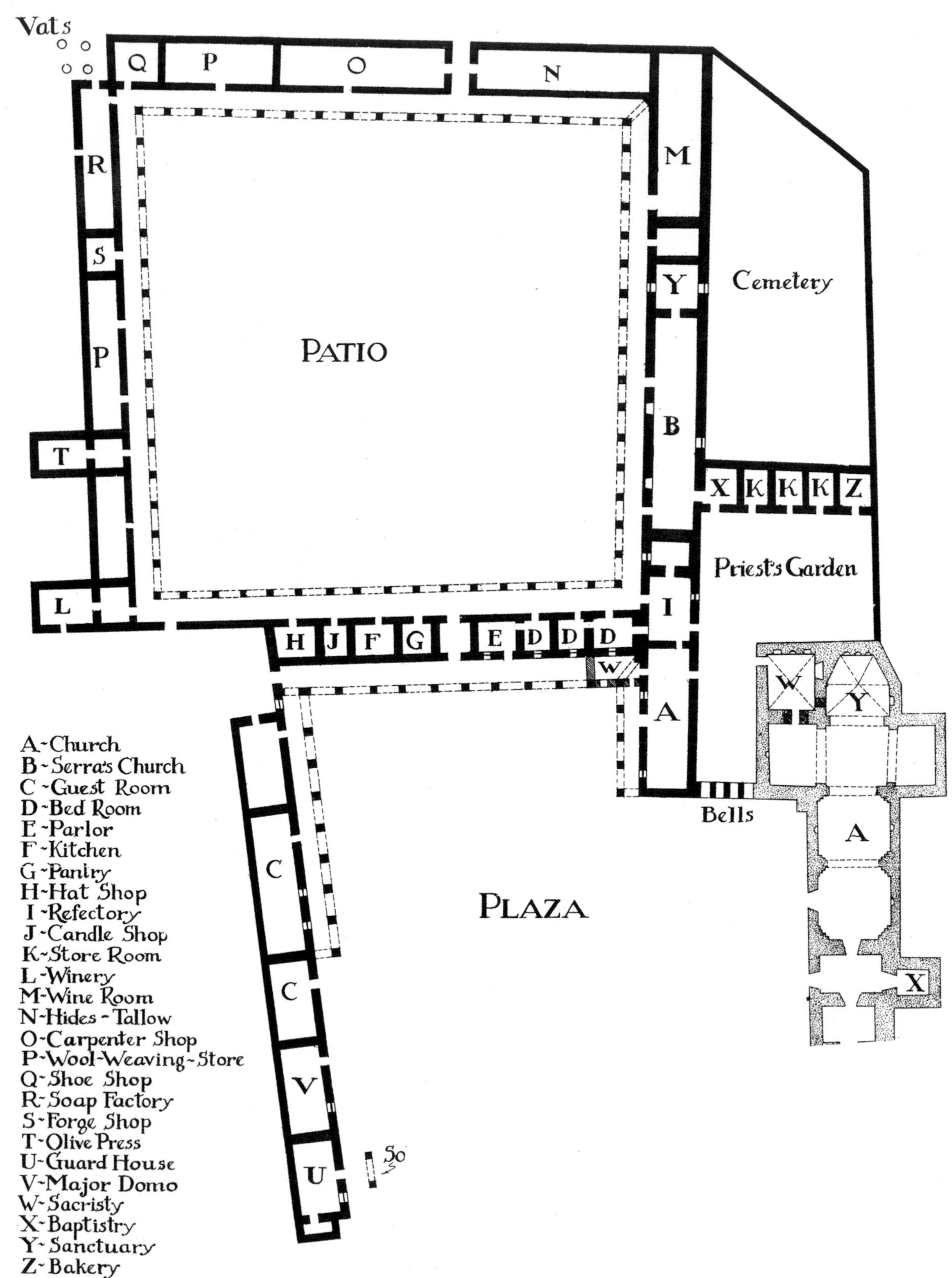

H. G. Maratta 1899. Irvine Museum

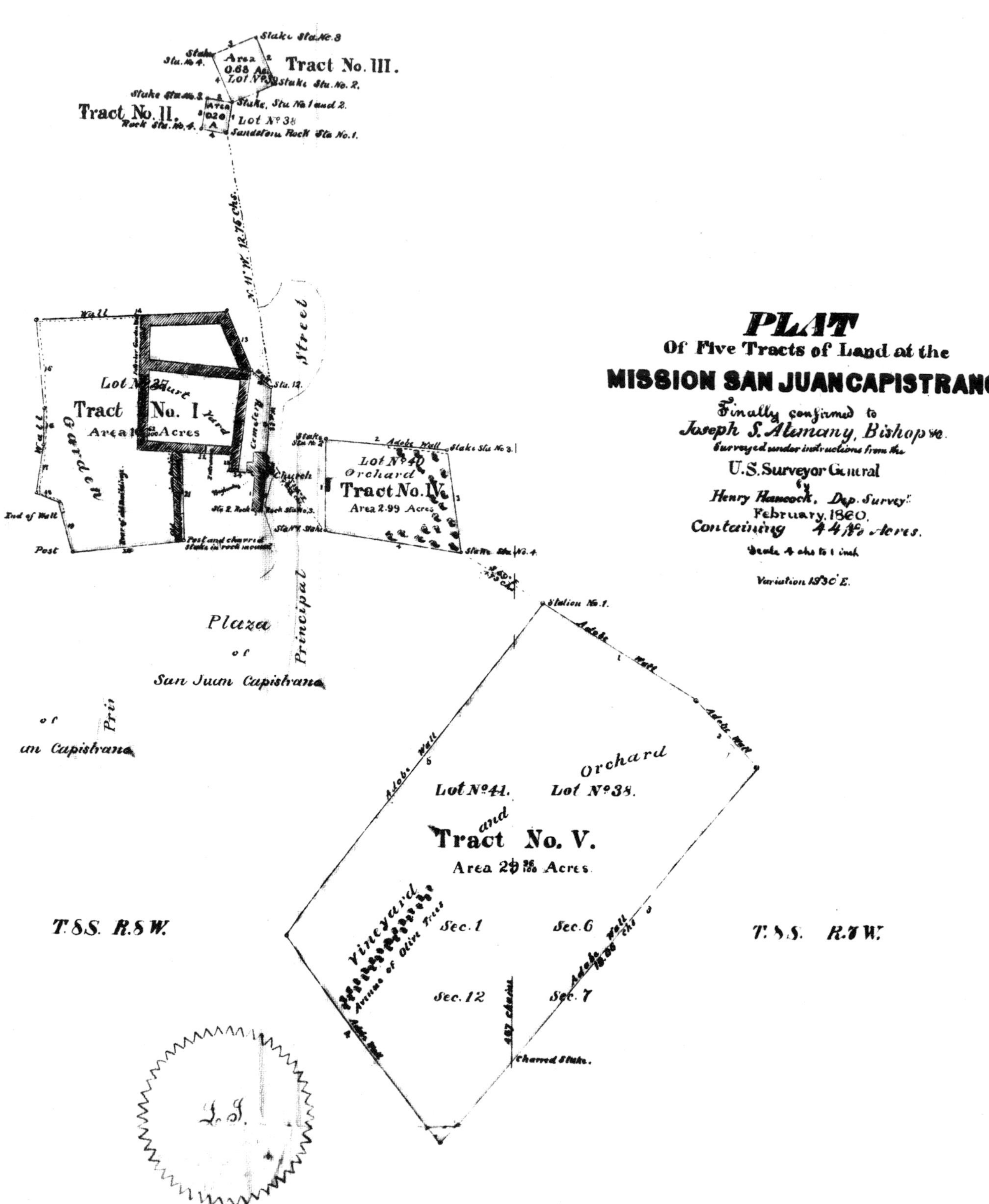
PLAT
Of Five Tracts of Land at the
MISSION SAN JUAN CAPISTRANO
Finally confirmed to
Joseph S. Alemany, Bishop &c.
Surveyed under instructions from the
U.S. Surveyor General
by
Henry Hancock, Dep. Survey.
February, 1860.
Scale 4 chs to 1 inch
Variation 13°30' E.
Tract No. III.
Tract No. II.
Lot No 38
Tract No. I
Tract No. IV.
Orchard
Area 2.99 Acres
Street
Principal
Plaza
of
San Juan Capistrano
Church
Cemetery
Garden
Wall
Adobe Wall
Lot No 41.
Lot No 38.
Orchard
and
Tract No. V.
Vineyard
Avenue of Olive Trees
Sec. 1
Sec. 6
Sec. 12
Sec. 7
T.8S. R.8W.
T.8S. R.7W.
Charred Stake.
Station No. 1.
Post

1860 Survey

Fred Behre and John Gutzon Borglum, 1894. Irvine Museum

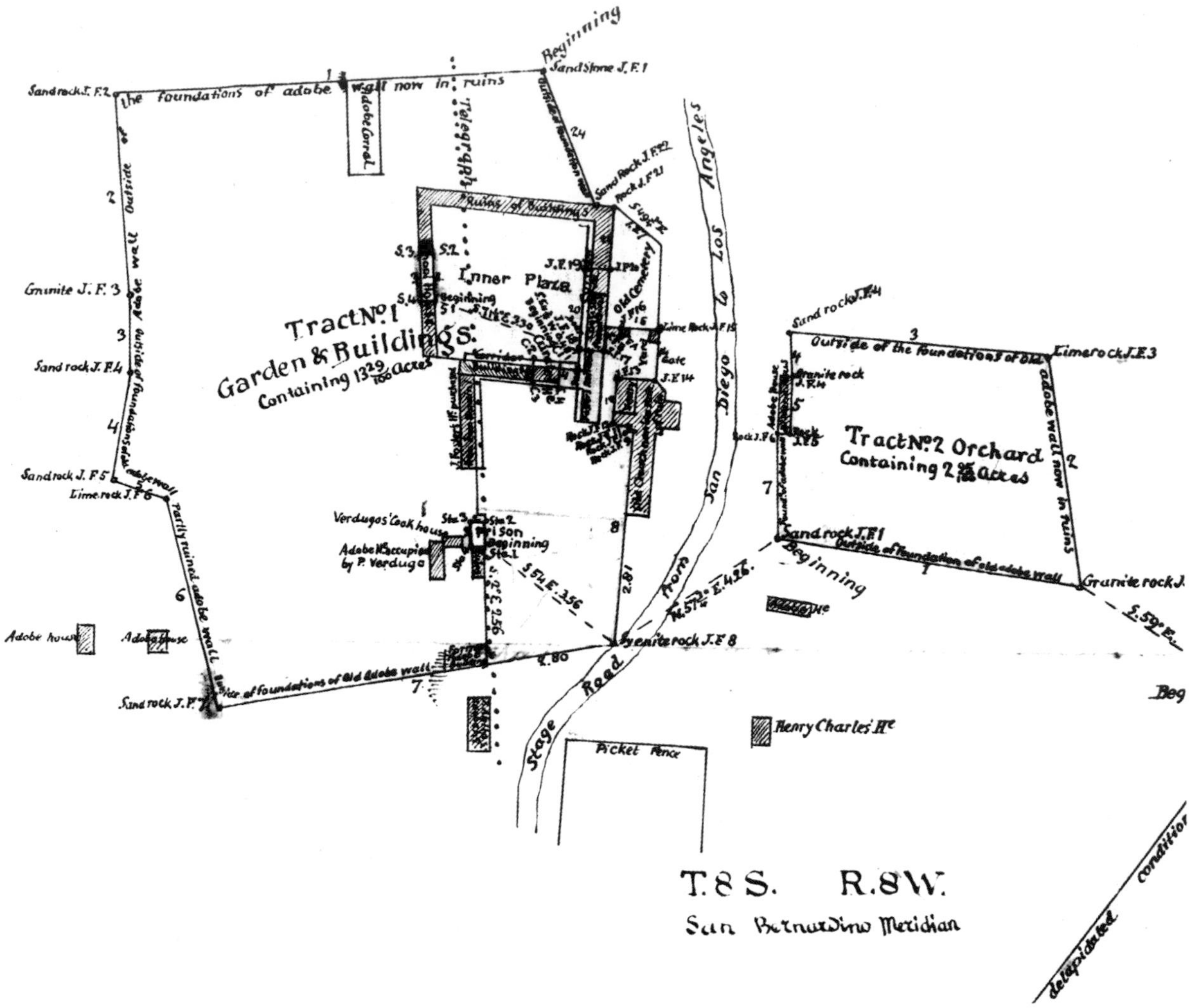

Fields of San Juan

Helen Duke

Soldier's barracks

South wing. Padres Quarters

Entrance Plaza Fountain

Post Card Views c. 1930s

Fountain of the Four Evangelists

Inner Courtyard: Serra chapel view from the fountain

West wing shops - Mission Museum

Inner courtyard : North wing

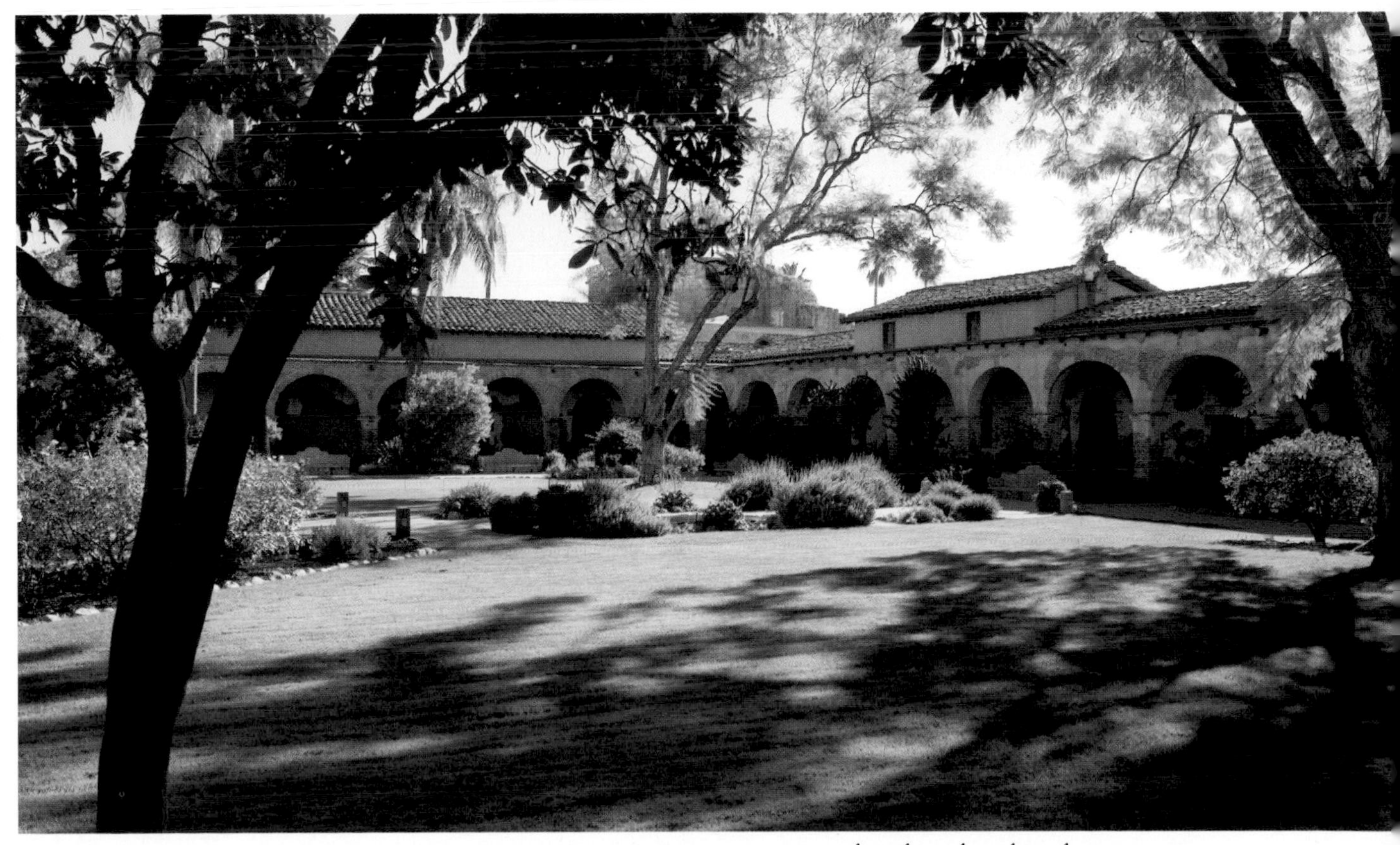

Inner courtyard : Chapel and Padres Quarters

Life at the Mission

Acagcheme Nation Juaneños

The Indians around San Juan Capistrano were primarily of the Acágcheme Nation. Those that were converted to Christianity and were baptized became Mission Indians and were simply called Juaneños. They came from many different villages, called rancherias – some large, some small, some close, and some quite far away.

Much of what we know historically about the Juaneños is second hand and from the perspective of a Spanish missionary. We might know even less if it hadn't been for the Spanish government which sent out a questionnaire (interrogatorio) to its American Colonies in 1812. This questionnaire covered thirty-six different topics regarding the backgound, habits, beliefs, customs, strengths, weaknesses, and attitudes of the Indians in their "pagan" state as well as in their current status as Mission Indians. The combined responses from all of the missions then existing provide an important overall view of Indian life that might otherwise not be available.

Prior to this, something of the Spanish attitude may be seen by the way the Spaniards referred to them. They called the Indians gentiles and themselves gente de razon, or "people of reason." Of course, they must have regarded the Indians as rational human beings, albeit of a primitive class, otherwise they would not have baptized them. They regarded all of them as children who needed to be watched, taught, corrected, and cared for as a parent cares for their children. It was very much a patriarchal attitude.

Communications were understandably slow and it wasn't until August 8, 1814, that Father Gerónimo Boscana answered the interrogatorio for Mission San Juan Capistrano. Although the reply is in his handwriting, it was made in consultation with his fellow missionary, Father José Barona. The answers are consistent with the responses of the other missions, but are considered very brief by comparison. Perhaps this is because Father Boscana had only been at the Mission for several months. He was, however, an experienced missionary and had served in the California Missions since 1806.

The Franciscan historian, Father Zephyrin Engelhardt, has provided this translation:

"The settlement at San Juan Capistrano, comprises, besides the two missionaries, only full-blooded Indians and six soldiers of the guard with their families.

"Among themselves, the Indians speak their own language. Many of them understand a little Spanish, but not perfectly.

"They love their wives, provided they please them or have children. The children however, receive no education from them at all. Besides instructing them in the Doctrina and in their obligations, the missionaries teach them agriculture and the mechanical arts, so that the Indians may learn to maintain themselves and become civilized.

"The Indians are very vacillating. Hence we cannot say whether or not they harbor any affection for the Europeans.

"In their savage state, they have neither characters nor ciphers for writing, since their whole knowledge is from tradition. They are fond of learning to read and write in our characters; but it is more from curiosity than through eagerness.

"These Indians are poor and wretched; wherefore we find meekness and submissiveness to be their principal characteristics.

"They have many ridiculous superstitions which are difficult to understand.

"In this Mission we use a short catechism, comprising what the natives must know as Christians. It is translated into their own language, along with the Acts of Faith, Hope, Charity, and Contrition.

"It is known that in their savage state they worship a large bird similar to a kite (milano), which they rear from its nest with the greatest care. Regarding it they have many erroneous ideas.

"The manner in which they contract marriage is as follows: The lover will send a representative, always a relative, to the parents of the girl, asking that they let her become his wife. If they consent, he will send her presents in the shape of beads, seeds, or other trifles that are in vogue. Then, for some days, the girl serves in the habitation of the groom, and if she pleases him, they are regarded as married. Of course, this refers to the Indian only in the savage state.

"Their methods of healing are simple. If the malady is external, such as wounds or tumors, they use various herbs, which after being crushed and roasted in an oven, are applied. If the malady is internal, they employ superstitious practices, as sucking through a quill, etc.

"They distinguish the seasons of the year by means of the trees watching them when they begin to bloom, to bud, and to lose their foliage, as also from the time when seeds and herbs may be gathered. They count the months by the moon, and the hours by the sun.

"At the Mission, the neophytes are given their regular meal in the morning, at noon, and in the evening. The pagans, however, have no stated hours, for they eat at all hours as long as they have something.

"These Indians do not use any fermented drinks, not in their pagan state, either, as far as is known. All are very fond of getting drunk, however; for if they can find any liquor, they do not stop drinking until they are overcome.

"We do not know whether they adore moon and sun. When they see the new moon however they make a great outcry to show their satisfaction. If there is an eclipse of the sun or moon they shout at the top of their voice at the same time beating on the ground or on hides or mats with sticks, in order to manifest the pain they feel.

"The Indians preserve all the customs of their forbears. But by prudence and zeal the Christians are gradually weaned from them. Regarding their race, nothing could be discovered.

"At their burials, or rather after them, they retire and weep, and perform a dance at which they practice all their superstitions and brutalities.

"As to fidelity in their dealings, they may be compared to the Chinese.

"As the father of lies has dominated them so many centuries, he has imbued them with the habit of lying to such a degree that they cannot say the truth without first lying; for almost always they say the opposite of what they have in mind.

"We can say nothing about their dominant vices.

"They do not refuse to share what they have with their friends or relatives.

"The Indians are very irascible and nourish hatred a long time. In their savage state, they would revenge themselves even by killing; but we do not know whether these Indians ever offered human sacrifices.

"As the Indians live in community, they are all equally rich and poor. They recognize only a capitan, whom they call such.

"Apparently, these Indians never heard music, for they do not cultivate it; nor have they in their pagan state any musical instruments whatever. On the other hand, our music pleases them exceedingly, above all the pathetic and melodious, vocal as well as instrumental music. It must be observed that they easily learn to play any instrument, no matter what it may be.

"We believe that there are very few who have the faintest idea of Eternity, Hell, and Heaven. In their pagan state, they appear to be materialists.

Indian dancers

"At this Mission, we use the same kind of clothing in form and texture as is used at the other missions, men and women."
Father Josef Barona Father Gerónimo Boscana.

Perhaps this "Interrogatorio" spurred a lingering interest in Father Boscana's mind about the nature of his Indian charges. Eleven years later, in November of 1825, he finished an extensive study of their background in a manuscript entitled "Chinigchinich (pronounced Ching-ee-ching-itch), an Historical Account on the Origin, Habits, and Tradition of the Indians at Mission San Juan Capistrano Called Acagchemem Nation."

Following Boscana's death in 1831, José de la Guerra at Santa Barbara, who took care of the Franciscan financial affairs, found the manuscript and entrusted it to Alfred Robinson who later included it in his own work, Life in California, which was first published in 1846.

It is clear that Father Boscana must have spent considerable time patiently questioning the Capistrano Indians about their traditions and their beliefs. They must have trusted him to open up as much as they did about their past practices and views. They had no written tradition, so Boscana's efforts provided an invaluable insight into their lives which otherwise might have disappeared.

We don't know for whom he intended this manuscript and, because it ends so abruptly, it may have been unfinished. He presents what he was told by the Indians he questioned, but his personal conclusions are sometimes harsh. Of course, they don't pretend to represent every missionaries views, just how he personally perceived the Indians entrusted to his ministry.

Father Boscana didn't realize in his own time what an important task he had undertaken. His work is the only contemporary account of Mission Indians produced by a California missionary. Anthropologists and ethnologists have long considered his account a unique and significant contribution to California Indian Studies.

Fr. Geronimo Boscana

CHINIGCHINICH;

A

HISTORICAL ACCOUNT

OF THE

ORIGIN, CUSTOMS, AND TRADITIONS

OF THE INDIANS AT THE MISSIONARY ESTABLISHMENT

OF ST. JUAN CAPISTRANO, ALTA CALIFORNIA;

CALLED

THE ACAGCHEMEM NATION;

COLLECTED WITH THE GREATEST CARE, FROM THE MOST INTELLIGENT AND BEST INSTRUCTED IN THE MATTER.

BY THE

REVEREND FATHER FRIAR GERONIMO BOSCANA,

OF THE ORDER OF SAINT FRANCISCO,

APOSTOLIC MISSIONARY AT SAID MISSION.

TRANSLATED FROM

THE ORIGINAL SPANISH MANUSCRIPT,

BY ONE WHO WAS MANY YEARS A RESIDENT OF ALTA CALIFORNIA.

NEW YORK:
PUBLISHED BY WILEY & PUTNAM,
No. 161 BROADWAY.
1846.

The Mission Routine

Life at the mission was somewhat similar to life in a Franciscan community. There was a regular routine providing a more or less constant balance and rhythm of prayer, work, play, and rest. Mission Indians lived at the mission, close at hand and removed from the distractions and temptations of their former life in the wild.

Each day at sunrise the mission bell would call everyone to begin their day with prayer. The adults gathered at the church where one of the padres celebrated Mass while the other led the Indians in prayer and the recitation of the Doctrina.

The Doctrina

The Doctrina was a short catechism of basic prayer and Christian doctrine based on a book of religious instructions written by Father Bartolomé Castaño. The padres at every mission were to teach this to the Indians without changing it in any way. By constant repetition and on-going explanations, it was hoped that it would become a guiding force in the life of each Christian Indian. It consisted simply of the Sign of the Cross, the Our Father, the Hail Mary, the Apostles' Creed, the Act of Contrition, Acts of Faith, Hope, and Charity; the Confiteor, the Ten Commandments; the Precepts of the Church; the Seven Sacraments; the Six Necessary Points of Faith, and the Four Last Things. Following this, everyone sang a hymn of praise, the Alabado.

Indian builders

The Alabado

Alabado y en salzado Sea el Divino
Sacramento, En quien Dios Oculto
Asiste De las Alamas el sustento,
Y la limpia Concepcion, De la Reina de los
Cielos, Que quedando Virgen
Pura, Es Madre del Verbo Eterno.
Y el Bendito San Joseph, Electo
por Dios In menso, Para Padre estimativo
De su Hijo el Divino Verbo.

Breakfast and Work

After the Doctrina, it was time for breakfast. Cooks at the community kitchen, the pozolera, prepared atole in large kettles. Atole was a kind of gruel made of roasted and ground corn or grain. Everyone received their share which was served in bark or earthen vessels. Before eating they would make the sign of the cross and pray the Bendito, grace before meals. The young men and girls ate their meals in their own separate quarters.

Following breakfast it was time to get busy with the work of the day. The padre called them together and announced their assignments. The tasks were many and varied.

Fields for the main crops needed to be cleared, plowed, sewn, and harvested. Grain had to be threshed and the corn husked. Ditches and water works had to be prepared for irrigating the crops and bringing water to the mission for drinking, cleaning, and washing. Work in the gardens, orchards, and vineyards was needed to supply the communities' vegetables and fruits. Workers had to protect and tend to the livestock – cattle, horses, mules, burros, sheep, goats, pigs, and chickens. Cattle had to be pastured, branded, rounded up, and, sometimes, slaughtered for food. Hides needed to be stripped and tanned for leather and fat rendered for tallow. Building construction and maintenance required workers in the carpenter and blacksmith shops. Some had to cut and transport timber; some had to procure stones for foundations; and others mixed mortar, formed adobe bricks, and fired pavers and roof tiles. Workers were also needed for the various mission shops that produced saddles, shoes, hats, soap, candles, and clothing. These diverse chores changed during the year according to the seasons and current needs.

The padres and professionals brought up from Mexico trained and supervised the Indians and often worked side by side with them.

Indian women took care of tending the children, cooking, cleaning, and other tasks such as carding, spinning, weaving, sewing, and tailoring. A matron taught and supervised the young girls and single women in these and other occupations.

The government provided for the missions as they were just starting out. However, it was expected that each mission become self-sufficient as soon as possible. Of course, as the mission population became larger, more food, clothing, and other needs had to be taken care of. Growth in the mission community required growth in productivity. Everyone who could had to work. Those missions that enjoyed a surplus shared with the others that needed help. In this way the mission chain became a community of communites.

Noon and Afternoon

The Angelus Bell closed the morning work session and called all to dinner. This time the meal was pazole, a kind of stew made with meat, beans, lentils, garbanzos, or whatever the season dictated. After dinner there was free time – time for a siesta or whatever someone chose to do.

At two o'clock it was back to the work of the day. This continued until five o'clock. At this time everyone gathered in the church for prayer and the recitation of the Doctrina. During this hour a padre usually gave a short religious instruction explaining some part of the Doctrina. Sometimes this was given in Spanish and sometimes in Indian. After this they all sang again the Alabado.

Supper and Sleep

At six o'clock it was time for supper, which was another serving of atole as in the morning. Afterwards, the Indians were free to do what they wanted, "so long as decency and Christian modesty were not offended." The Poor Souls Bell rang at about eight o'clock. The mission gates would close an hour later. It was time to call it a day.

Life at the mission was in sharp contrast to the daily freedom the Indians had enjoyed in the past. However, the Fathers knew the natives would have to change their ways if they were to survive in the new civilization coming upon them. The Indians would need to know the skills of ranching and farming to live in such a world. They would have to learn new skills and master various trades. A more disciplined way of life would make them more productive and successful in the busy, competitive way of life that the Old World was bringing to the New. Life at the mission was designed to prepare them for the larger changes that destiny would demand.

The evening star. Sydney Laurence. Irvine Museum

Mission dancers.
Janine Salzman

Provincia de } *Californias.* { Misiones del Colegio ~~Nueva California~~ de S. Fernando.

Noticia de las Misiones que ocupan los Religiosos del Colegio Apostolico de San Fernando de Mexico, de los años de 1792, y 1793.

Misiones.	Ministros.	Sinodos. De Real Hacienda.	Sinodos. De Obra pia.	Sinodos. Total de sinodos.	Indios. Hombres.	Indios. Mugeres.	Indios. Total	Españoles y gente de otras clases. Hombres.	Españoles y gente de otras clases. Mugeres.	Españoles y gente de otras clases. Total	Total de Almas.
San Diego	2	0	800	800	8	62	0	0	10	0	872
					8	69		0	09.		878.
S. Juan Capistrano	2	0	800	800	8	22	0	0	00	0	822
					9	69.		0	00		969.
S. Gabriel	2	0	800	800	1.2	19	0	0	08	0	1.227.
					1.2	25.		0	08		1.233.
S. Buenaventura	2	0	800	800	6	08	0	0	33	0	641.
					5	08.		0	04		512.
Santa Barbara	2	0	800	800	5	04	0	0	11	0	515.
					5	41		0	12		553.
La Concepcion	2	0	800	800	5	10	0	0	08	0	518.
					5	46.		0	01.		547.
S. Luis Obispo	2	0	800	800	7	36	0	0	02	0	738.
					7	51.		0	00		751.
S. Antonio d. Pad.	2	0	800	800	1.0	74.	0	0	05	0	1.079.
					1.1	42.		0	00.		1.142.
La Soledad	2	0	800	800	1	18	0	0	00	0	118
					2	13.		0	00.		213.
San Carlos	2	0	800	800	8	00	0	0	08	0	808.
					8	35.		0	11.		846.
Santa Cruz	2	0	800	800	1	55.	0	0	00	0	155.
					2	33.		0	00		233.
Santa Clara	2	0	800	800	1.0	01.	0	0	06	0	1.007.
					1.0	62		0	06.		1068.
N. P. S. Francisco	2.	0	800	800	6	22	0	0	04	0	626.
					7	11.		0	04		715.
Totales en. 1792. .	26	0	10400	10400	9.0	31.	0	0	95	0	9.126.
Existian en. 1793. .	26	0	10400	10400	9.6	05.		0	55.		9.660.
Diferencia.	0	0.	0.	0.	5	74.	0.	0	40.	0.	534.

Por la Demostracion anteced.te se acredita q.e en el año de 1793 se aumentaron los Indios de las Misiones en 574, y disminuyeron en 40 los Españoles, permaneciendo los Ministros, y Sinodos en el mismo estado.

En los dos años se verificaron 602 Matrimonios de Indios; 2.699 Bautismos, y 1.399 Difuntos. Asimismo huvo 39 Matrimonios de Gente de razon, y se bautizaron 180.

En

❱ *A report prepared for the missionary college in Mexico city*

IV The Bells of Capistrano

"The mission bells will ring, the chapel choir will sing, the happiness you bring, still lives in my memory."
Leon Rene, When the Swallows Come Back to Capistrano

First Bells

The welcome sounds of the first bells of San Juan Capistrano have long ago faded into history. There were two of them, borrowed from San Gabriel. That mission was the storage place for goods and equipment destined for the founding of Mission San Buenaventura. This had been postponed several times because of the lack of sufficient soldier guards. San Gabriel decided to use the San Buenaventura bells while loaning its own bells to San Juan Capistrano. Why it did that is unclear. Perhaps, the San Gabriel bells were smaller, lighter, and easier to transport down to the Capistrano site.

When the founding party under Father Lasuén reached that site late in October of 1775, the bells – probably hung up on a branch – rang out the joyful announcement of the mission's beginning.

After just eight days, the bells fell silent and remained so for over a year. News that Mission San Diego had been attacked and burned forced the abandonment of Capistrano and a hasty retreat to the relative safety of the San Diego Military Presidio. The cumbersome bells, along with two heavy millstones, were buried and left to await a new beginning at a better time.

A year later, when calm had been restored and relative security assured, Father Junipero Serra and a new founding party returned to the site. He had the bells dug up and re-hung. In ceremonies marking the new beginning, the bells rang out again, happily announcing a sound and lasting presence. It was November 1, 1776.

How long these two bells served and what eventually happened to them is not known. It is certain that they are not the ones that are there now. Perhaps, the original ones were returned to San Gabriel and replaced by larger ones. Perhaps, they eventually broke and were recast into some other larger bell or bells.

Whatever their fate may have been, it is likely that they served the mission for quite a long time, perhaps, even up to the founding of the Great Stone Church in 1806. The ancient bells now at the mission were certainly used in that church.

Bells of the Great Stone Church

The bells of Capistrano still remaining at the Old Mission are well over two hundred years old and once hung in the belfry of its Great Stone Church. That tower was completely destroyed in the 1812 earthquake and no design plan has ever been found. Nevertheless, archelogical examination and accounts later related by the elder members of the community provide a description. The bell tower, situated at the front of the church and attached to its eastern, or right hand side, is estimated to have been about eighty feet high. Outside steps led up to the first of its three upper floors. Here the bell ringers stood while carrying out their scheduled duties. The bells are said to have hung on three levels: the largest bell at the top; the next largest was beneath it on the middle level; and two small ones graced the bells ringers station.

San Vicente

The largest bell is named San Vicente. Its greenish hue reveals its large copper content. The crown shape of its top indicates that it is a crown, or royal bell. Such bells are often thought to have been gifts of the King presented through his Viceroy. The outside barrel of the bell bears the inscription:

"VIVA JESUS SN VICENTE ADVON DE LOS RRS PS MIROS F VICTE FUSTR IF JN SANTIAGO 1796."

This translates as "Praised be Jesus and Saint Vincent. In honor of the Reverend Fathers, Ministers Fray Vicente Fuster and Fray Juan Santiago." The date reveals that it was cast twenty years after the mission was founded. It was obviously intended for the Great Stone Church whose construction began the following year. Fathers Fuster and Santiago are the padres who made its plans. The bell's name, San Vicente, probably honors the patron saint of Father Vicente Fuster, who was the senior missionary.

It seems highly unlikely that these two humble Franciscans would have dedicated the bell to their own honor. It seems more probable that the bell is a gift for the church by some kind and generous donor who wished to also honor these two hard-working missionaries. It is of particular interest that this is the only bell in the California Missions known to bear the names of its ministers.

San Juan

The second largest bell is named San Juan, possibly for the patron of the mission, San Juan Capistrano. It's may also be named after St. John, the patron of Father Santiago who signed his name Juan Norberto de Santiago. If this is the case, it would certainly fit in with the San Vicente which took its name after the patron of Father Vicente Fuster.

This bell carries the inscription:

"AVE MARIA PURISIMA ME FESIT RUELAS I ME YAMO SAN JUAN 1796,"

which means, "Hail Mary Most Pure. Ruelas made me and my name is San Juan." Like its big brother it is a crown bell, only smaller and with a lighter tone. It bears the same date as the San Vicente and is so similar to it that it seems likely that both were made in the same place by the same person whose name, Ruelas, is inscribed on the bell.

Paul Ruelas is believed to have been a bell maker at the Zimopan Foundry in the State of Hidalgo, Mexico. During the period of 1795 – 1809, his name also appears on bells found at Missions San Gabriel, San Francisco, Santa Clara, Santa Barbara, San Carlos, and San Juan Bautista.

San Antonio

The larger of the two small bells is the San Antonio, named after Saint Anthony of Padua, a great Franciscan saint. It was cast eight years after the large bells, but still two years before the construction of the Great Stone Church was finished. It is inscribed: "AVE MARIA PURISIMA SAN ANTONIO 1804." This translates as "Hail Mary, Most Pure. San Antonio, 1804."

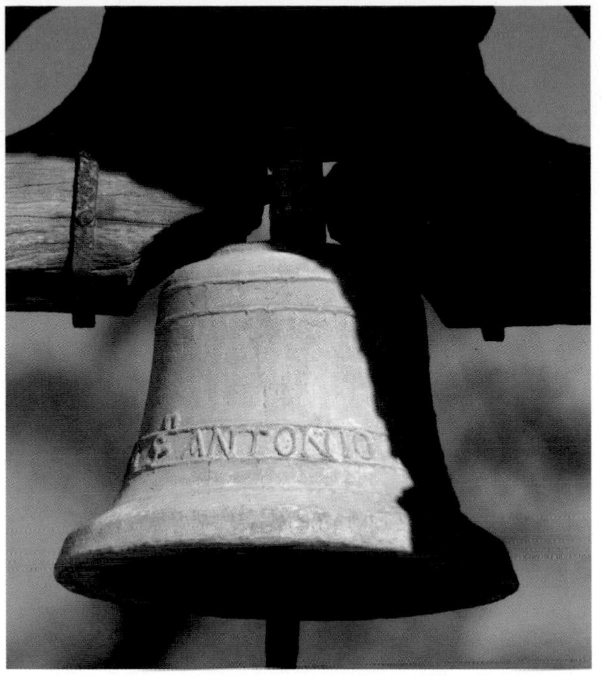

San Rafael

The smallest bell, San Rafael, is named after Saint Raphael the Archangel. It was also cast in 1804 and is the smaller twin to the San Antonio. It is inscribed: "AVE MARIA PURISIMA SAN RAFAEL 1804," which translates as "Hail Mary, Most Pure. San Rafael, 1804."

These two bells, along with the San Juan, share the salutation to Mary, Most Pure. It seems probable that this was because every day these bells called their listeners to pray the Angelus, a popular prayer to Mary, the mother of Jesus.

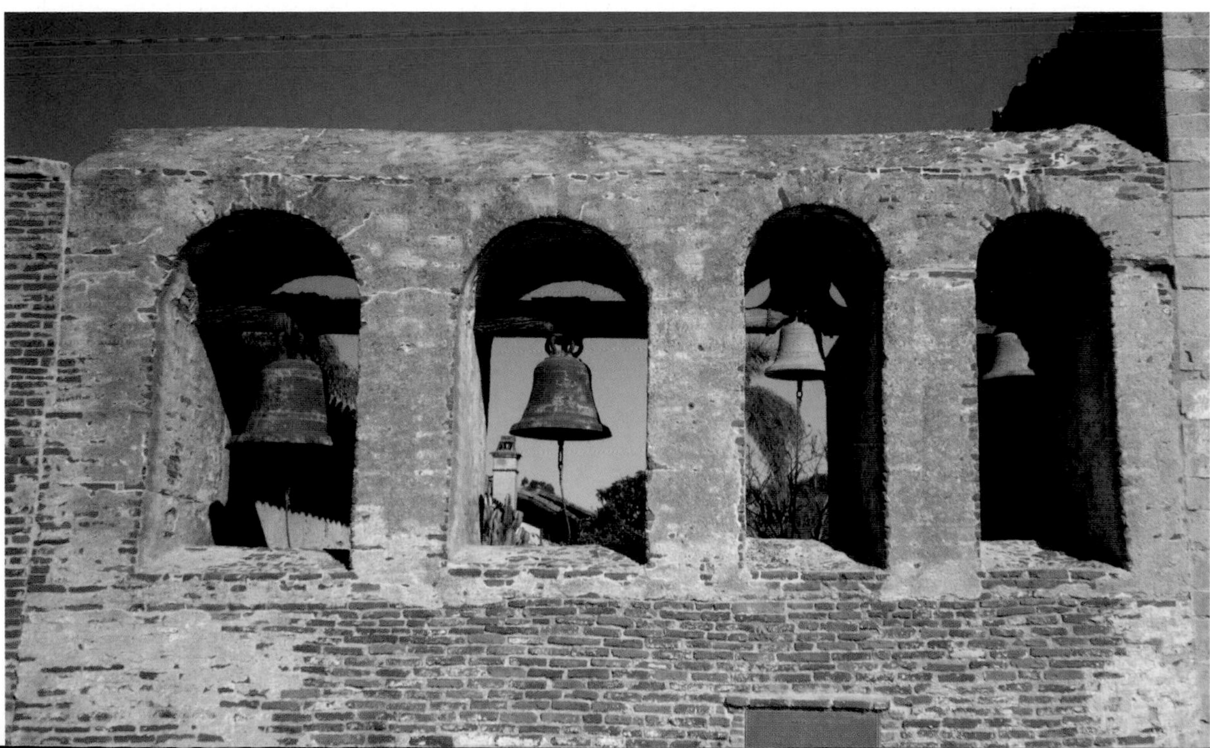

The Campanario

Following the destruction of the Great Stone Church in 1812, a bell wall, or campanario, was built to accommodate the mission bells. It is made of mortar and both adobe and fired bricks. The bells hung in their separate arches attached to wooden beams with rawhide straps. Strong, carefully braided rawhide ropes attached to the bell clappers, or tongues, extended down to the front of the campanario where the bell ringers stood.

Bells Rule the Day

"I will wake the dawn. I will give thanks to you among the peoples, Lord. I will ring out your praise among the nations."
(From Psalm 56)

The bells of Capistrano called its Juaneños to prayer, meals, work, and sleep. At sunrise they announced the beginning of a new day and called the community to begin it with prayer. An hour or so later the breakfast bell called everyone to their hot bowel of atole. They didn't have to hear that bell twice. Sometime later, it summoned them to the mission patio where everyone was given their assignments and then went off to work. A bell rang again at noon commencing the Angelus prayer and calling everyone to dinner and siesta or free time. At two o'clock the work bell declared it was time to go back to the day's labor. The five o'clock bell ended the work and called everyone to return – a summons that met with eager obedience. It was time for late afternoon prayer and devotions. At six o'clock, the bell rang again for the Angelus prayer and, then, supper and free time. And at eight o'clock the De Profundis, or Poor Souls bell reminded all to say a prayer for the deceased. The larger bells were generally rung for prayer and worship while the smaller bells were used to announce the times for work, meals, and rest. At nine o'clock the mission gates were closed and everyone retired for their night's rest.

Naturally, the schedule changed on the weekends and holy days. The Indians seldom worked on Saturdays unless there was some urgent need. On Sundays the divine mandate to rest was observed religiously. And at special times, such as the visit of a dignitary, the bells were rung to joyously celebrate the occasion. This pattern of bell ringing was the same at all the missions.

How did they know it was time to ring the bells? Every mission had a sun dial to help them know the time. Some had mechanical clocks. Records for 1774 indicated that Father Serra even had an alarm clock.

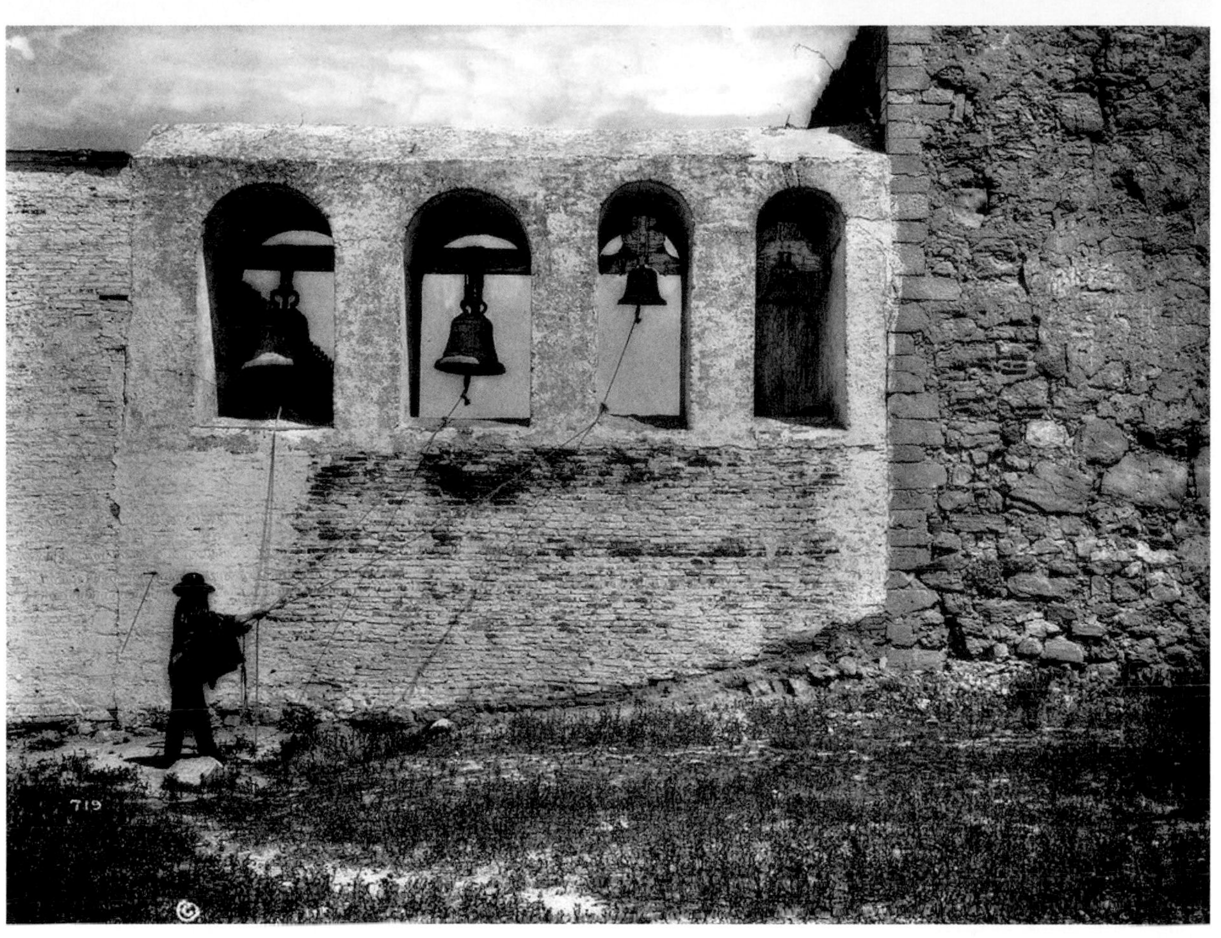

Campanario c. 1880s

Method

The method of ringing the bells varied from mission to mission. Some of the difference was due to the number and size of the bells, which varied from place to place. Each mission started off with two bells, one larger and one smaller. Although the time and purpose for ringing the bells remained uniform throughout the missions, the method employed by an Indian bell ringer or sacristan at one mission might well be different from that of another at a neighboring mission. This was especially true when more bells were added.

At Mission San Juan Capistrano, the Misa Grande (High Mass) on a Sunday or Feast Day was proclaimed by a joyful peal of the bells. This was a sequential clamoring of all four bells rung by two bell ringers. There were three "repiques" made at half-hour intervals. A "repique" consisted of each bell rung sharply in succession. After the first "repique", a single loud stroke was given to the largest bell, the San Vicente. After the second "repique", it received two such strokes and, after the third, three. Immediately afterwards, the "clamores " followed – about twelve heavy strokes on the San Vicente and then on the San Juan.

The Angelus prayer was announced by three strokes repeated three times on the Ave Maria bells, followed by nine strokes in succession. During Easter time the Regina Coeli prayer replaced it. For this three strokes were made slowly on the large San Vicente bell and then the rest at decreasing intervals. This was followed by several strokes made quickly. Afterwards, the same pattern was repeated on the next largest bell, the San Juan.

When someone passed away at the mission, it was announced by a slow, sad tolling of the bells. If the death occurred after the evening Angelus bell, the tolling was deferred to the next morning at daybreak.

The method of tolling announced whether it was the death of a man, woman, or a child. The death of a man was announced by tolling the large bells three times followed by the little bells. The death of a woman was made known by tolling the two large bells twice along with the ringing of the smaller ones. And a child's death was announced by just ringing the little bells, the San Antonio and the San Rafael.

Bell Ringers

It was an honor for a Mission Indian to be chosen as a bell ringer. He had to be responsible, intelligent, and carefully trained. No record has been found listing them all, but in the relatively modern period we know of some. The last full-blooded Juaneño Indian, José de Gracia Cruz, old "Acu," was a bell ringer in the first quarter of the 1900s. He learned the method of ringing from his father who also held that post. Later on Jesus Aguilar, Ramon Yorba, Paul Arbiso, Steven Chavez, and Michael Gastelum have shared these duties.

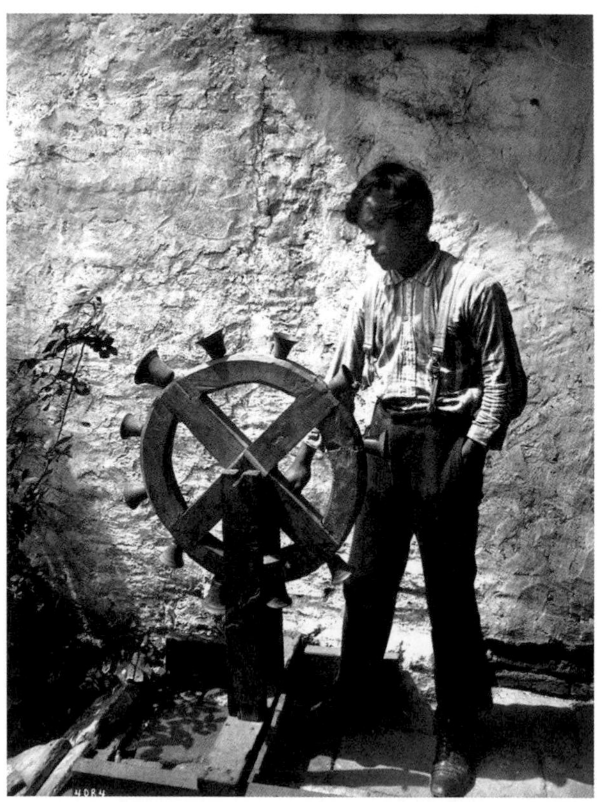

Gloria Bell Wheel

Other Bells

Old timers remembered that there were also single bells stationed outside the padres' quarters and the military barracks. This is probable since this was common at the other missions. They were call bells used as needed for whatever purposes were required beyond the normal routine of the day. Possibly hand bells were also used, especially for calling the children for religious instruction and other activities.

Small altar bells would have been used announcing the beginning of Mass and at various times during its celebrations. A large bell wheel still remains among the mission's artifacts. It was used during Holy Week, joyfully accompanying the Gloria. A matraca, not a bell but a wooden clapper, replaced the bell at the sad, solemn times during Holy Week.

c. 1890s

c. 1890s

› *Building the Sacred Garden 1920*

Fr. St. John O'Sullivan

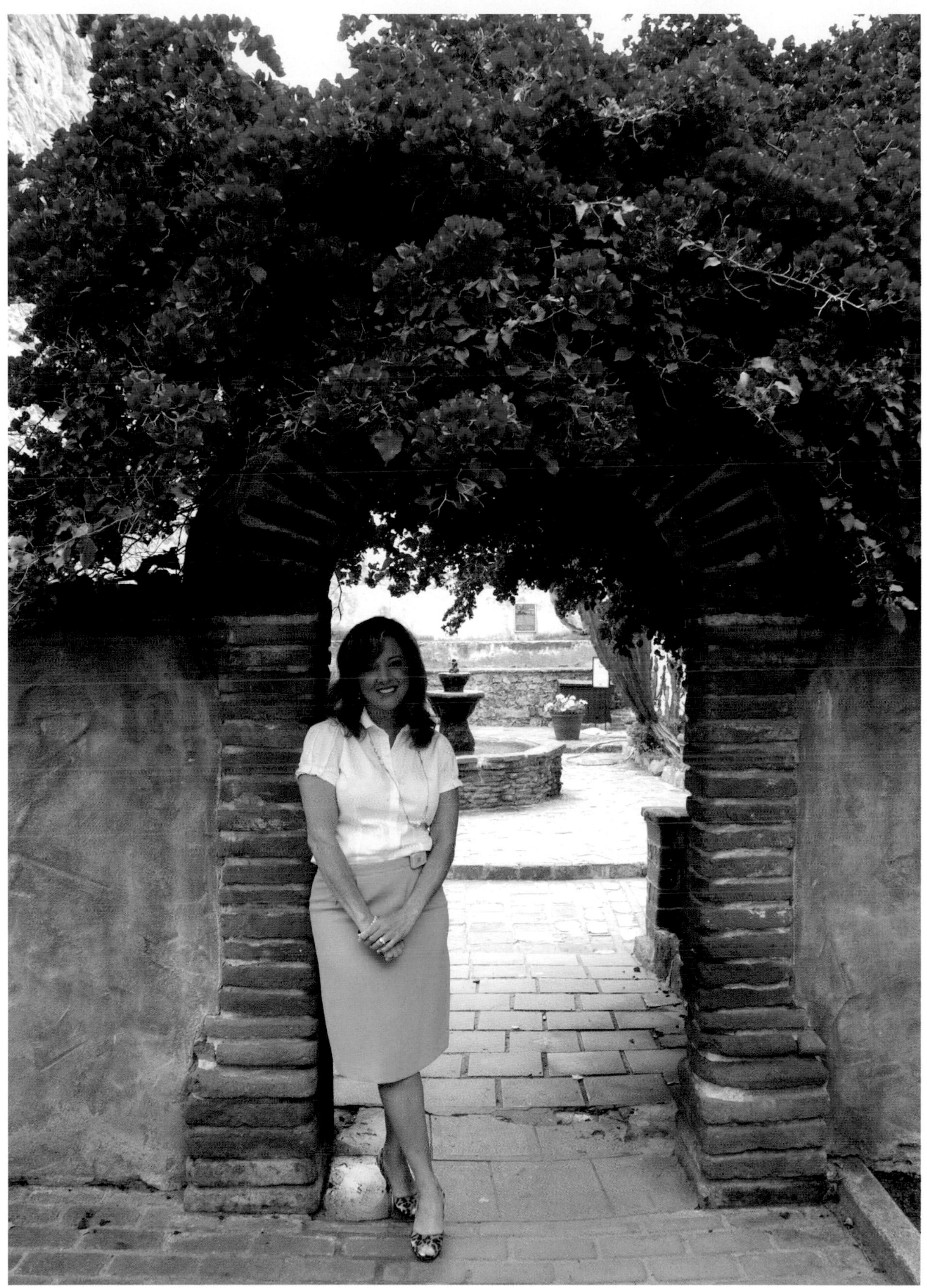

Mechelle Lawrence Adams. The Mission's executive director

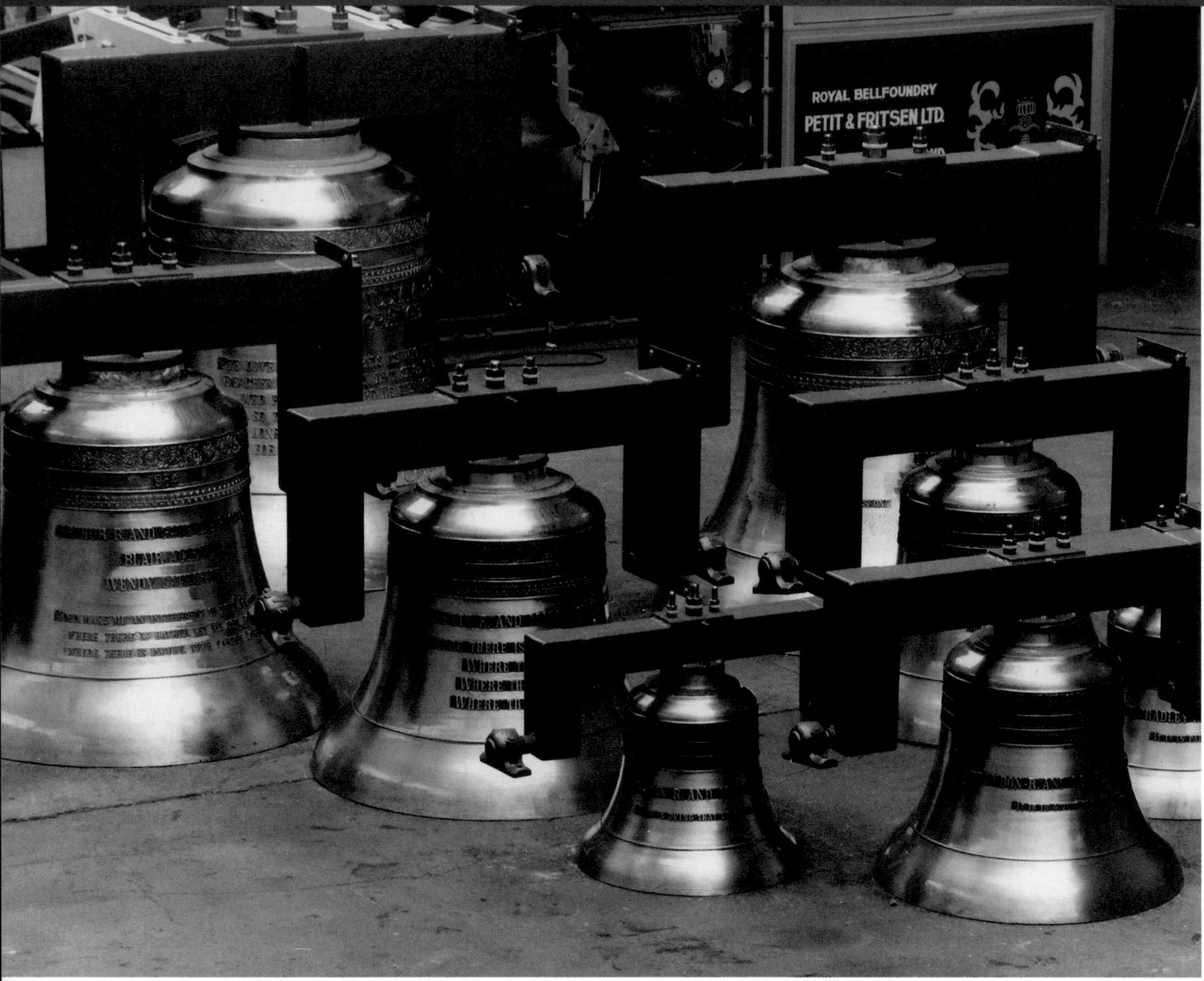
ROYAL BELLFOUNDRY
PETIT & FRITSEN LTD.

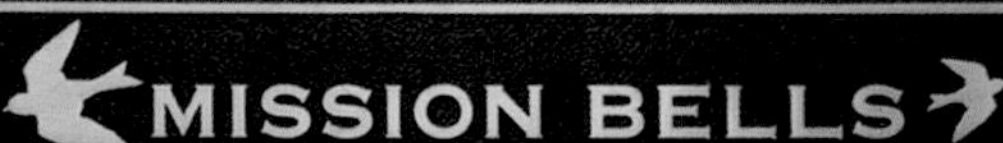

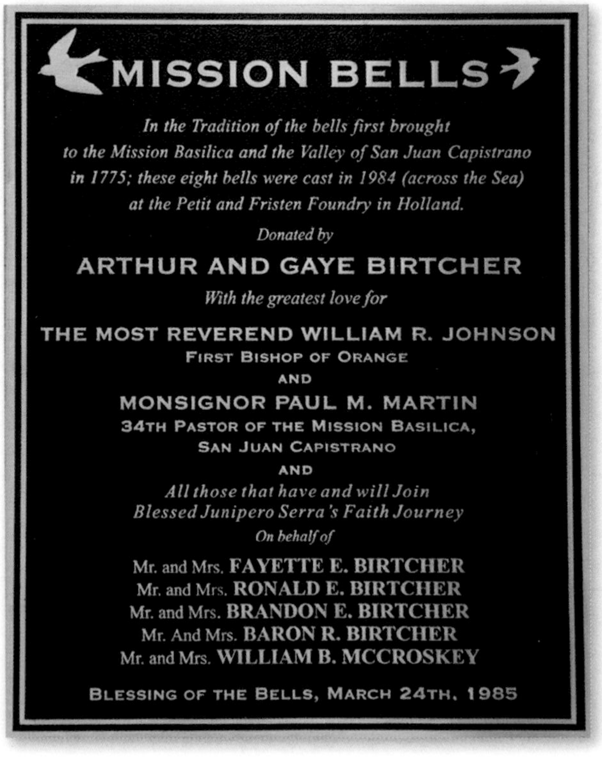
MISSION BELLS
In the Tradition of the bells first brought
to the Mission Basilica and the Valley of San Juan Capistrano
in 1775; these eight bells were cast in 1984 (across the Sea)
at the Petit and Fristen Foundry in Holland.
Donated by
ARTHUR AND GAYE BIRTCHER
With the greatest love for
THE MOST REVEREND WILLIAM R. JOHNSON
FIRST BISHOP OF ORANGE
AND
MONSIGNOR PAUL M. MARTIN
34TH PASTOR OF THE MISSION BASILICA,
SAN JUAN CAPISTRANO
AND
All those that have and will Join
Blessed Junipero Serra's Faith Journey
On behalf of
Mr. and Mrs. FAYETTE E. BIRTCHER
Mr. and Mrs. RONALD E. BIRTCHER
Mr. and Mrs. BRANDON E. BIRTCHER
Mr. And Mrs. BARON R. BIRTCHER
Mr. and Mrs. WILLIAM B. MCCROSKEY
BLESSING OF THE BELLS, MARCH 24TH, 1985

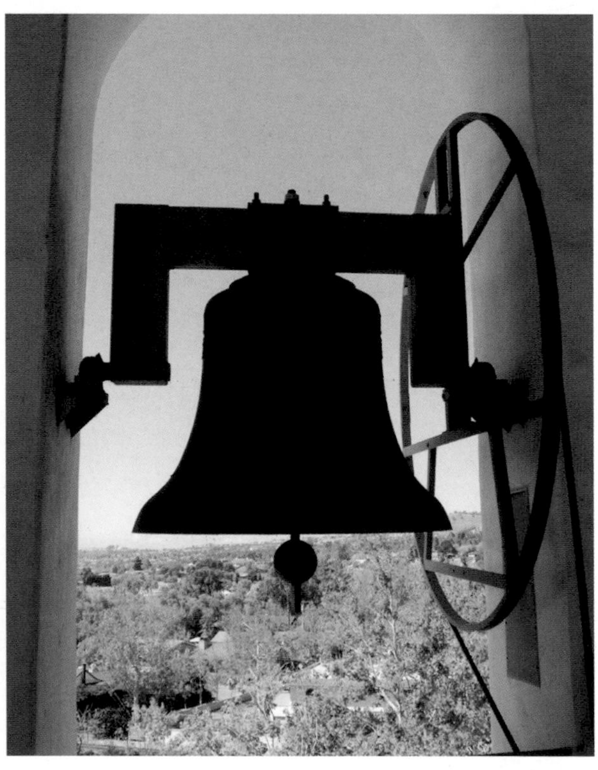

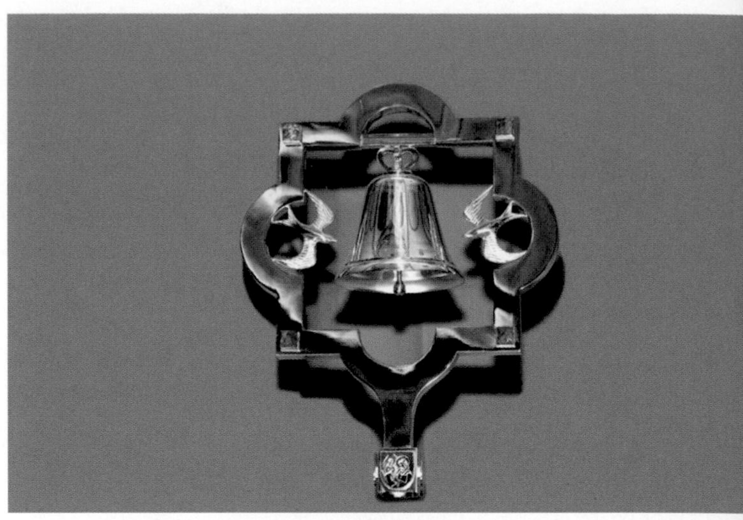

MISSION BELL PARK
CITY OF SAN JUAN CAPISTRANO 1980

Gene Autry

Bicentennial

V The Serra Chapel
Father Serra's Church

The church of San Juan Capistrano later became known as Father Serra's Church, or, more simply, Serra's Chapel. It acquired this name because it is the only remaining church in the California Missions where Father Junipero Serra celebrated Mass and administered the Sacrament of Confirmation. It also has the distinction of being the oldest surviving building in California.

The Serra Church was not the first church of San Juan Capistrano. The first church was built on the mission's original site, which it occupied for nearly two years. That church would have been primitive, made of plastered wooden poles and having a simple, flat roof of tules, or brush. It was understandably humble, yet made holy by its purpose.

Because of water failure at that place, the mission was relocated to its present site on October 4, 1778. During the previous summer an adobe residence and a "partly adobe" church had been prepared for occupancy. That church was about 55 feet long and 11 feet wide. It had a flat roof covered with jacal (brush).

Later that month, on October 23, the Feast of San Juan Capistrano, Father Junipero Serra celebrated Mass there, baptized, and administered confirmation. Where exactly that building was located is not certain. It seem likely that it was on the same site as its successor, the present Serra Chapel, because by 1782 when the new "permanent" church was built, there were already 64 burials in the cemetery which was next to it.

The new church was larger and more substantial. It had thicker adobe walls and was longer and wider. The main entrance was on the western or patio side, although another entrance was available from the south end. Together with its sacristy, the building was about

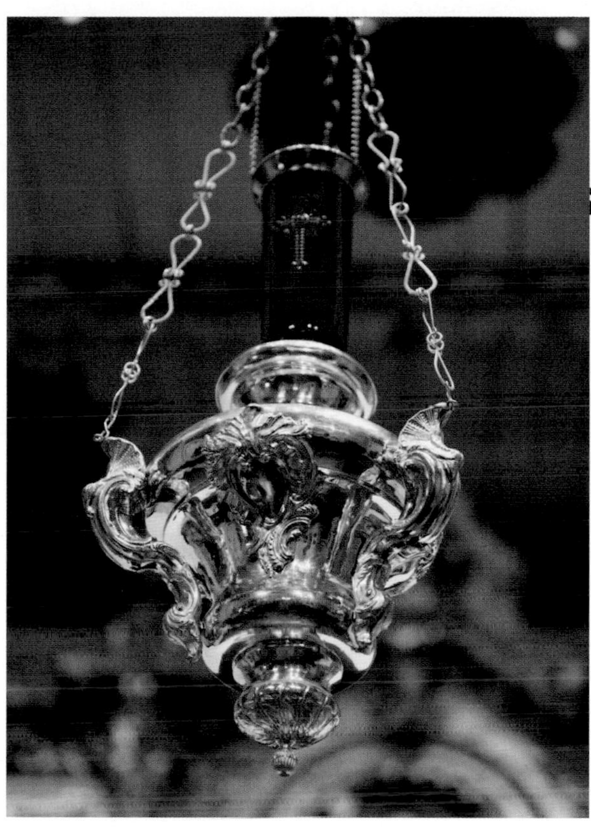

82 feet long and 19 feet wide. As with the temporary church, it too had a flat roof covered with jacal. In this improved, but still modest structure, Father Serra again celebrated Mass and administered the Sacrament of Confirmation on successive days: October 12, 13, and 14, 1783.

The year 1790 saw major changes to the Serra Church. The mission was then fourteen years old. Its Indian population had increased to 765, nearly 400 more than when the church was first built. The church was nearly doubled in size. The old sacristy was incorporated into the church and a new sacristy built. The walls were raised higher and a new tile roof replaced the old flat one. On the west entrance side, facing the patio, a colonnade was provided with a tile roof and pillars of brick and mortar. On the eastern, or cemetery side,

two small rooms were added, perpendicular to the church. One of these, the one attached directly to the church, was probably used as the baptistery. Three years later, in 1793, a third room was added to the extension.

The Serra Church served the mission for twenty-four years. In it the padres celebrated Mass, proclaimed the Word, preached, instructed, held devotions, baptized, distributed Holy Communion, heard confessions, presided at weddings, conducted funerals, and all the other things that make a church sacred.

Every year San Juan Capistrano Mission continued to grow. As early as 1797, the population was over a thousand and still increasing. That year plans were made for a new, much larger and more substantial church – the Great Stone Church. Nine years later, in 1806, it opened with great celebration and fanfare. The Serra Church was dwarfed in its shadow and was no longer needed. What use was made of it at the time is not known. Nevertheless, its life as a church was far from over.

In 1812, a great California earthquake shook down the Great Stone Church. It was beyond repair. The shocked community returned to the humble Serra Church. It once again embraced its mission family and continued as their house of worship through the rest of the Mission Period and well beyond that.

In the early 1830s secularization brought an end to the mission system and inaugurated a period of rapid decline. Nevertheless, even as other buildings went to ruin, the Serra Church persevered. That doesn't mean it was immune to the indignities of aging. By 1867 the roof was so dilapidated that part of it over the sanctuary area collapsed. Padre Joseph Mut, who had only been there a year, had neither the money nor any other means to restore this ruined part. He solved the problem by building a new adobe wall that was raised up to meet the remaining intact roof. This restored the church to its purpose, but had the effect of leaving the old sanctuary with the entombed remains of the missionary fathers outside the shortened church. Ironically, the 1782 church, enlarged in an earlier more

Serra Chapel c. 1880s

prosperous time, was now – eighty-five years later – returning to its smaller size.

Nevertheless, this determined little church did not surrender to its setbacks. It bravely remained home to the Lord and His small Capistrano community. It served them as it had served their parents and grandparents and others before them. Countries had changed; missionaries had come and gone; buildings had gone up and come down; new generations replaced the old ones; but the Serra Church abided, a faithful home and center to its people.

Window to the Past

There are two accounts of activities in the Serra Church that give us a glimpse of religious services held there in olden times. The first is a description of Doña Palonia's wedding. It was described by the bride and published many years later in *Capistrano Nights*, written by Father St. John O'Sullivan and Charles Saunders. The second is found in the memoirs of Mary "Mollie" Sheehan who lived in San Juan Capistrano as a young girl and helped out with services in the church.

Doña Palonia's Wedding

"There were many people there at the wedding; they came from far up the province, from Monterey and Santa Barbara and down near San Diego. The marriage took place in the old church, the one back of the mission which you must pass through the zaguán to reach – Father Serra's church. In the doorway of the church the padre (Father Rosales) met us and asked the first questions: 'Francisco, will you take Polonia here present for your lawful wife according the rite of our Holy Mother, the Church?" Then he asked me the same, and then we went farther into the church and joined hands. As soon as we did that the guns and small cannon that the men had got ready just outside the door went off, almost to deafen us, and the smoke came rolling into the church. And then we went up to the altar and mass was said, and we knelt under a large belt of flowers. Over my dress I had a white mantle of very fine silk, which covered my head also and hung down before my face. The only flowers I wore were three white roses in a row on the right side of my head. As we knelt we held large wax candles all covered with flowers. Six girls wearing crowns of white flowers stood with me and six with Francisco. For eight days there was merrymaking and feasting and then all returned to their homes. My great-grandmother gave me this advice: 'Palonia,' she said, 'if your husband says at midday it is midnight, you agree with him that it is midnight; and if at midnight he says it is midday, agree with him in that too!'"

[Note: Father José Maria Rosales was at the mission from 1850 through 1853.]

Wedding

Molly Sheehan Remembers

"We were not too busy to answer the invitation of the bells swinging in the campanario, or to follow the trail downhill to early morning Mass or vespers in the dusky chapel fitted up in the ruins of the old mission. Here, too, were colors rich and warm. The flickering sanctuary lamp and the lighted candles glowed on a great painting of the crucifixion on the wall behind the altar. The Stations of the Cross also were done in oils in intense colors. I was not capable of judging whether these were pictures of art, but they satisfied me. Padre Joseph Mut, himself a native of Barcelona, told me that the Franciscans had brought them long ago from old Spain.

We were the only members of the congregation that were not Mexican or Spanish. Men and women came to church in their picturesque native costumes: shirts or tunics of silk or damask, velvet breeches, lace mantillas, serapes striped with bright colors, and mangas with richly embroidered collars. Servants of the well-to-do spread rugs for their households to sit upon. The others squatted upon the bare floor. There were no pews or chairs. My father made a bench for us and we were the only ones in the congregation who did not sit upon the floor. Everyone sang. A Mexican orchestra – guitar, violin, triangle, tambourine, castanets – furnished the bizarre accompaniment for the hymns at Mass and vespers…

The Mexicans liked me. I was a Catholic. I sang in the mission-chapel choir. When Padre Mut bought an organ and tried to have that music substituted for the music of the Mexican orchestra, I played the organ. I met the villagers and the rancheros and their wives and children at church. They interested me and I enjoyed them. I learned to speak their language and so entered into their lives…

Padre Mut made plans also to have me take music lessons so that I would be able to play the organ, to direct the choir, and to help him in his endeavor to have music for church services more sacred in tone, more suited to the dim religious atmosphere of the antique mission chapel than the tinkling instruments the Mexican orchestra afforded; the señors with their guitars could transpose even the "Sanctus" into the sentimental lilt of a moonlight serenade."

[Note: Mary accepted the marriage proposal of Peter Ronan, her boyfriend from Montana. He came down to Capistrano to marry her and take her back with him They were married in the Serra Church on January 13, 1873.]

"We planned to approach the marriage sacrament at an early hour. I wore a pearl gray dress, one of the two new ones my stepmother and I had made. I wore with it a silver filigree chain with pendant cross, breast pin, and earrings to match – Mr. Ronan's gift to me; a plain hat purchased in Capistrano; and a sheer pink shawl, the gift of Mrs. McGrath…

I arose at daybreak. We were all quiet – our hearts were full. After I knelt and the received the blessing of my parents, we all embraced each other and then went our way quietly to the chapel in the ruins of the Mission of San Juan Capistrano where we were joined in the holy bonds of marriage by the Reverent Joseph Mut. The holy sacrifice of the Mass was offered for us and we also received special benediction. I will never forget the words addressed to us from the altar.

Molly Sheehan Ronan

'I know,' said the Padre, 'my dear young people, that you have complied with every rule of the Church, that you have received the holy Sacrament of Marriage in a state of grace, and I believe also that it is not any worldly motive that prompts you to marry, but pure and true love.'

How impressive and solemn everything seemed. None was in the church save the priest, my father, sister, brother, and Mrs. McGrath. Every sound echoed through the quaint old rooms, and the statues with their great black eyes seemed as if they were alive, standing there to bear witness to the vows we had made.

On entering the church I leant on the arm of my father, when leaving on the arm of my husband."

Charles Percy Austin

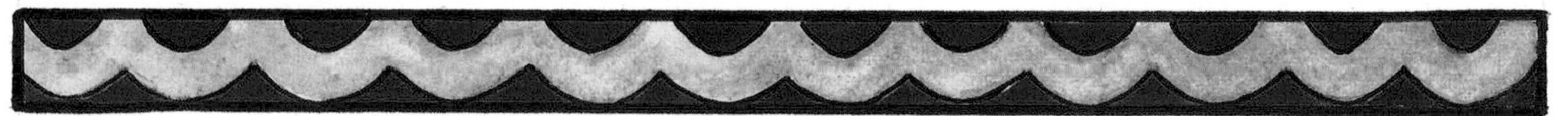

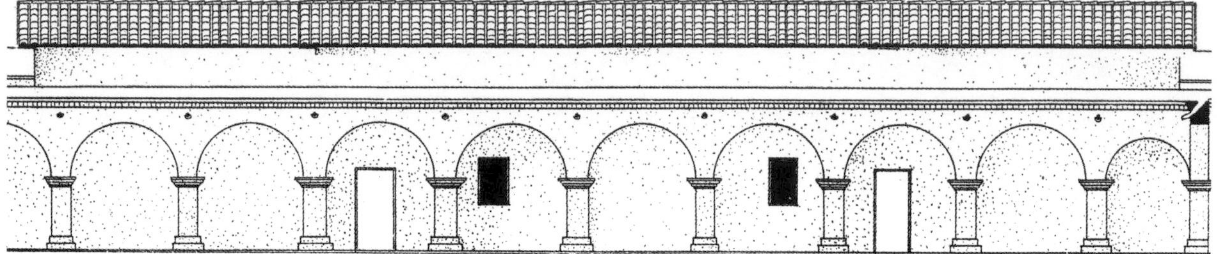

The Restoration

As time went on, some thought that the church had outlived its usefulness. In 1891 it was abandoned for a second time. The remodeled Sala – a smaller but better built structure – served as Capistrano's new place of worship for the next thirty-three years.

Although retired, the Serra Church stubbornly remained useful. The walls sagged; the roof drooped; but somehow it held together. In its venerable decrepitude, it became a storage shelter – a safe refuge for hay, barley, lumber, and whatever else needed keeping. As such, it patiently awaited someone with a restoring hand, a caring heart, and an eye to see beyond its obvious sad appearance and recognize it as an historic treasure.

One such man was Charles Fletcher Lummis, founder of the Landmarks Club. Seeking no profit for himself, he worked to raise awareness – and money – to save what was left of the Old Spanish missions. Fortunately, he started with San Juan Capistrano. In 1896, he focused the club's attention on the Serra Church. Rotting timbers threatened to give way. Water leaking into the building melted its adobe walls. Lummis had the old roof completely removed and restored with sturdy Oregon pine and carefully replaced tiles. His efforts saved the church and preserved it for better days.

Another such man was Father St. John O'Sullivan. He arrived at the mission in 1910 and almost immediately recognized the sad plight of the Serra Church, reduced to a storage building. He was determined to restore it to its original, sacred purpose. It took every bit of his charm and infectious enthusiasm. It took careful planning, professional assistance, and generous donations. And it also took fourteen years. It was worth the effort and the wait. In 1924 the extensively remodeled and re-enforced Serra Church once again became the Church of San Juan Capistrano. Its religious use and historic legacy continues to the present day.

One of the most important aspects of the 1924 restoration was the rebuilding of the sanctuary. This necessitated the removal of the 1867 adobe wall and the extension of the church northwards to its original length of 160 feet. That outside area had been almost completely ruined by its exposure to the elements. It had to be rebuilt from the ground up and a new roof placed over it. When this was completed, it restored the sacristy to its original location and once again incorporated into the sanctuary the remains of the missionaries who had been interred beneath its floor.

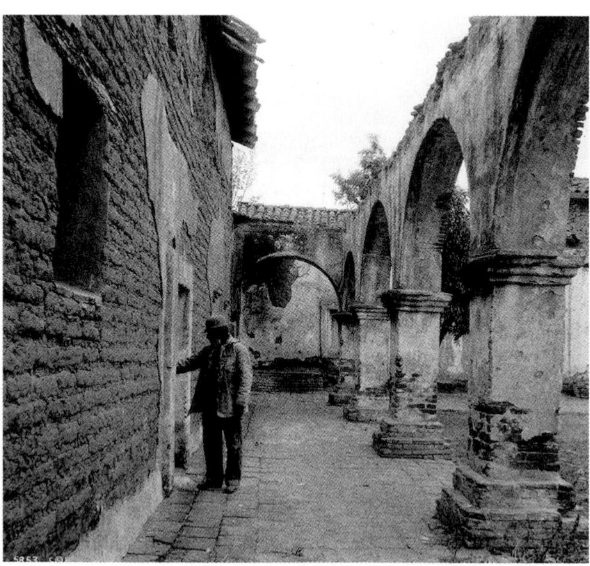

A custodian unlocks the Chapel c. 1890s

Exterior before restoration

Mortal Remains

Fray Vicente Fuster, the principal planner of the Great Stone Church, did not live to see its completion. He died on October 21, 1800. His body was placed in a crypt beneath the sanctuary floor in the Serra Church, where he had celebrated Mass and the Sacraments so many times. When the Great Stone Church was dedicated in 1806, his remains were solemnly transferred to the sanctuary of that splendid church which he had worked so hard to have built. However, when that building was destroyed by the 1812 earthquake, his mortal remains were once again placed in the original burial site in the center of the sanctuary of the Serra Church.

Fray Joseph Barona labored at the mission for twenty years. He had the sad task of presiding at the burial of thirty-nine of the victims killed by the collapse of the Stone Church. He himself passed away on August 4, 1831. His remains were placed in a crypt on the gospel (the right) side of the sanctuary, about midway between the altar and the Communion rail.

Fray Vicente Pascual de Oliva, one of the last of the Spanish missionaries, served at the mission from 1846 to 1848 – the beginning of the American Period. He died at the age of 68 on January 2, 1848. His remains were placed in a crypt on the epistle (the left) side of the sanctuary.

When the area was excavated for the 1924 reconstruction, workers also discovered the remains of Soledad Yorba de Avila. The fact that she had the privilege of being buried there indicates that this lady had earned a special place in the hearts of the mission padres and the Capistrano community.

Decorations

The colorful artwork decorating the interior of the restored Serra Church is based on authentic mission designs. Some of it was taken from painted decorations that had survived over the many years, especially the designs on the ceiling. Decorative ideas were also borrowed from original art remaining in the mission churches of Santa Ines and neighboring San Luis Rey.

Interior before restoration c.1920

1922

The Retablo

The most striking feature in the restored Serra Church is its retablo, often called the "Golden Altar." It is not actually the altar itself, but the elaborate decoration that incorporates it, adorns it, and focuses attention on it. This retablo, gracing the entire wall behind the altar is made of mahogany and ceder, hand-carved, and gold-leafed in the busy, baroque style favored in the 17th and 18th centuries. Such decorative pieces were found in the architecturally better churches in Spain and its more developed colonies. Of course, none of the California Missions – humble establishments on the Spanish frontier – would have been able to afford a retablo of this sort. However, it does not seem out of place. It fits in beautifully, almost as though it was always meant to be there. It seems an appropriate embellishment for such an historically important and sacred space.

The retablo is older than the mission itself, perhaps several hundred years old. Bishop Thomas Conaty, Bishop of Monterey-Los Angeles, purchased it in 1906. He intended it to be the centerpiece of a new cathedral to be called the Cathedral of Our Lady of Guadalupe.

The "Golden Altar" arrived in 396 pieces, packed into 10 shipping crates. Since the cathedral project was subsequently abandoned, the crates remained in storage in the basement of the rectory of old Saint Vibiana's Cathedral.

When Father St. John O'Sullivan sought permission to travel to Mexico to look for something special for the Serra Church, Bishop Cantwell, then Bishop of Los Angeles, suggested he use the old Spanish retablo which had come so far and not yet found a suitable home. It was not a difficult decision. Father O'Sullivan was delighted to accept the offer. He had it shipped down to the mission and placed in a shed specially built for it until the main construction work on the building was finished.

The task of assembling it went to Arthur B. Benton, a Los Angeles architect, and Sebastian Maas, a church decorator. There were, of course, some problems. Some pieces were missing and had to be custom made. Moreover, the retablo was too big. It was eighteen and a half feet wide by twenty-two and a half feet high. The sanctuary roof had to be raised higher than the rest of the church roof. This problem turned out to be a blessing because the difference between the two allowed for windows to be placed as a skylight. This allowed natural light to play on the highly ornamented gold leaf features of the ancient retablo. This presented a very pleasing contrast to the rest of the church, which is generally rather dark and somber.

The detailed features of the retablo call for a quiet meditation. There are spiraled, golden pillars adorned with grape vines. The pillars suggest a building, the celestial House of God. The clusters of grape suggest the wine that in the Lord's Supper becomes the Blood of Christ. The carved, polychrome figure of God the Father surmounts the whole scene. God the Son is depicted on a central crucifix as Christ crucified. An image of Mary as Our Lady of Guadalupe – original to the mission – is situated just above the tabernacle. Polychrome faces of more than fifty angels peek out from every aspect. And, as might be expected in a representation of God's house, various saints also grace the scene. High up in the central niche is the statue representing the mission's patron, St. John of Capistrano. On the right is St. Michael the Archangel and on the left is St. Peter the Apostle. On the lower level are the two great saints of Assisi: St. Francis, on the left, and St. Clare, on the right. With all of these features, the whole retablo becomes an inspiring sight as well as a religious instruction for all who contemplate it.

God the Father

St. Peter

St. Juan Capistrano

St. Michael

St. Francis

Our Lady of Guadalupe

St. Clare

St. Joseph Shrine

Mary Queen of Heaven

› *Sacred Heart of Jesus*

› *Our Lady of the Pillar*

› *Cardinal Timothy Manning. Bicentennial Mass November 1, 1976*

St. Ignatius Loyola

St. Dominic

I › *Jesus is scourged.*

II *Jesus carries the Cross.*

III *Jesus falls the first time.*

Stations of the Cross

 *Jesus meets his mother.*

 *Simon of Cyrene helps Jesus.*

 *Veronica wipes the face of Jesus.*

VII *Jesus falls the second time.*

Jesus meets the women of Jerusalem.

IX *Jesus falls the third time*

Jesus is stripped of his garments.

Jesus is nailed to the Cross.

XII › *Jesus is crucified.*

XIII › *Jesus is removed from the Cross.*

XIV › *Jesus is entombed.*

San Juan Capistrano

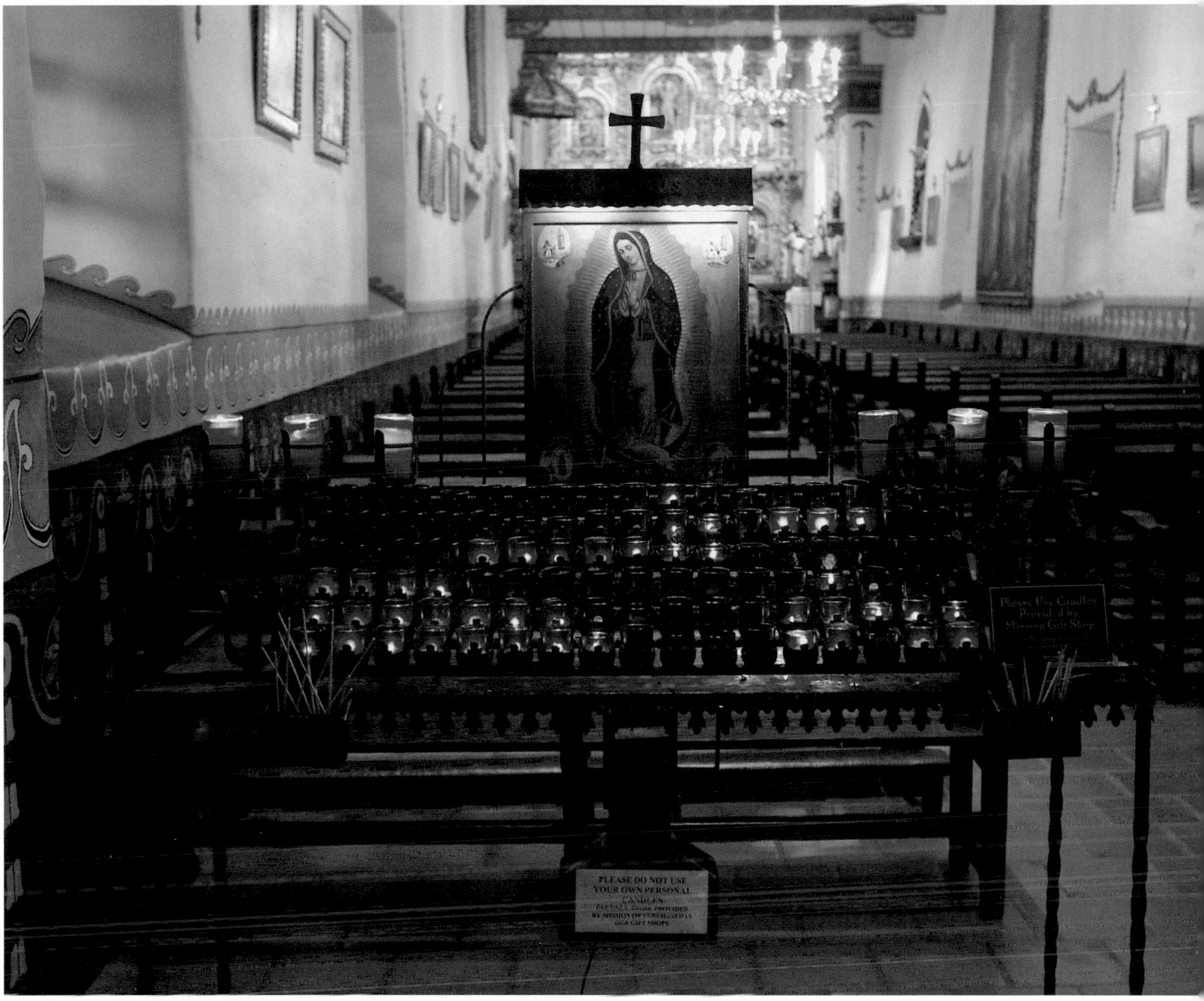
PLEASE DO NOT USE
YOUR OWN PERSONAL
CANDLES

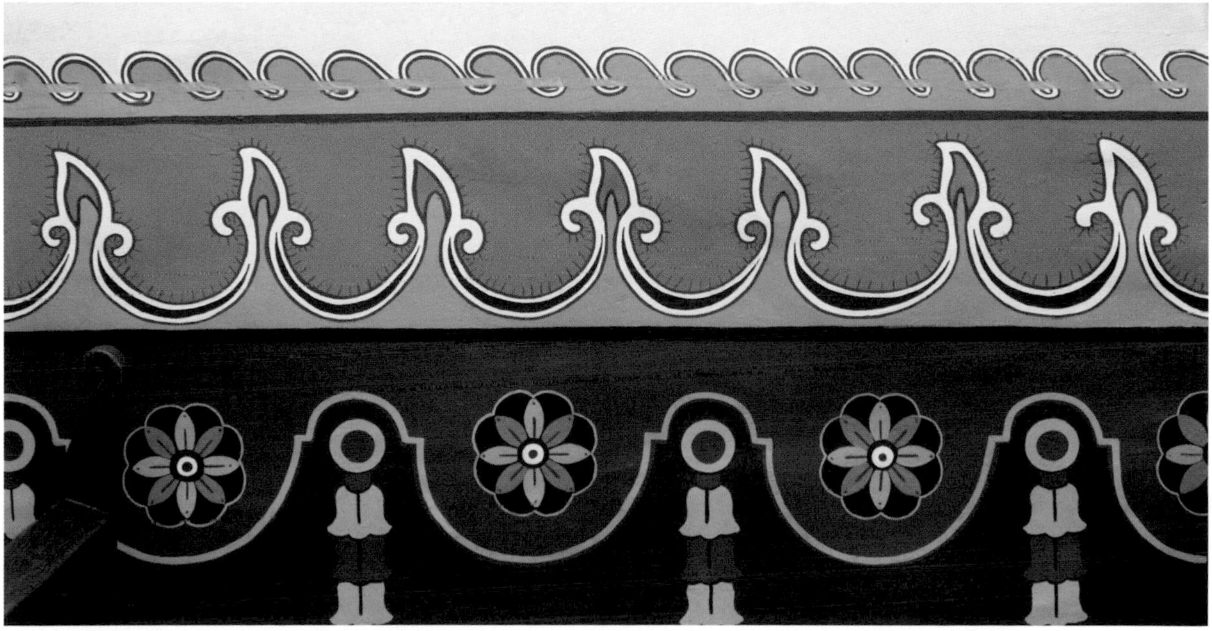

Chalice

Crucifix and Candelabra

› *Altar cards*

› *Censer*

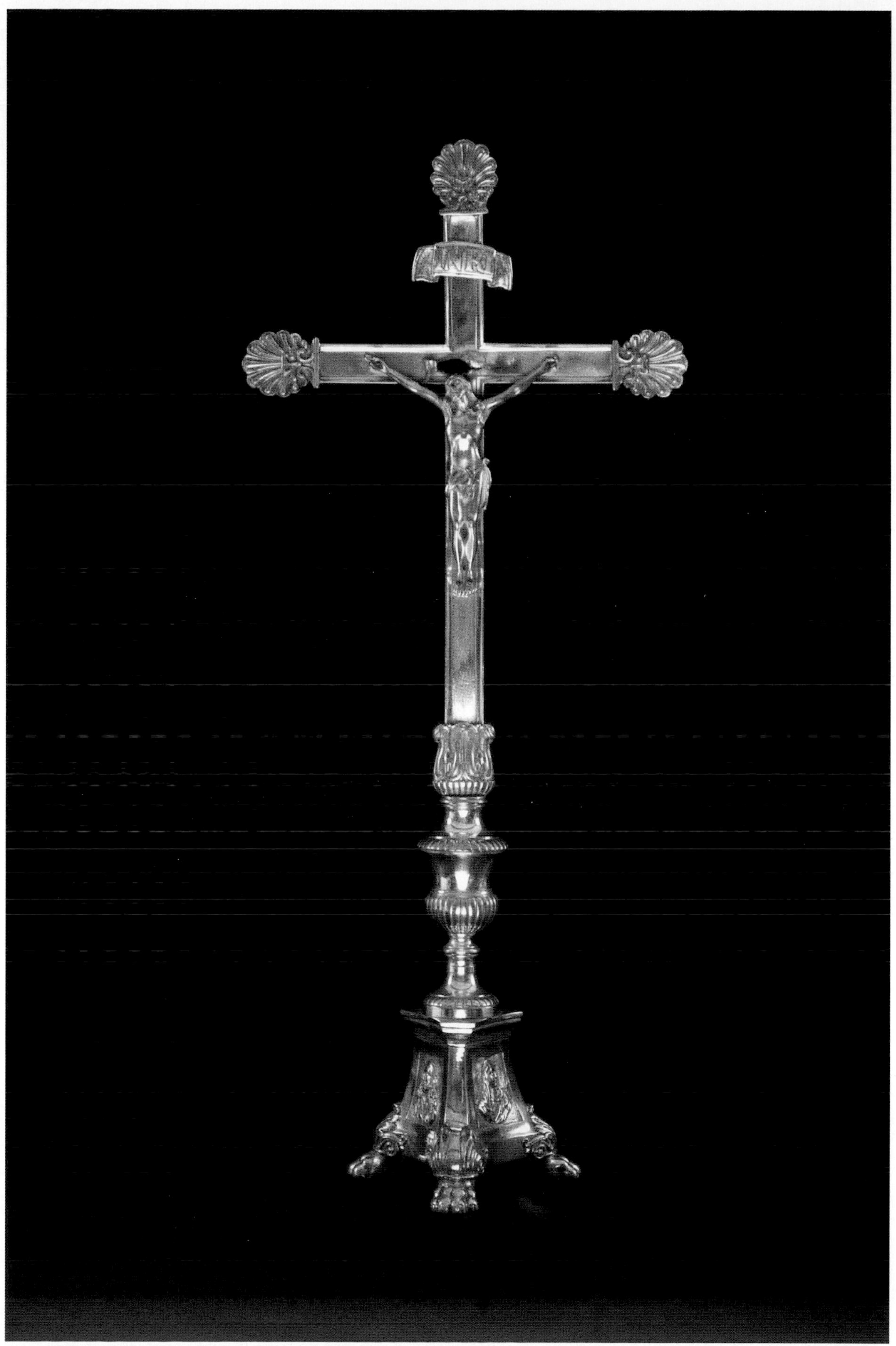

Crucifix

› *Green Vestment*

Funeral Vestment

Gold Vestment

Holy Water Vessel

› *Original Mission Registers : Baptisms, Marriages, and Burials*

Father Zephyrin Engelhardt, Franciscan historian, studies Baptismal register

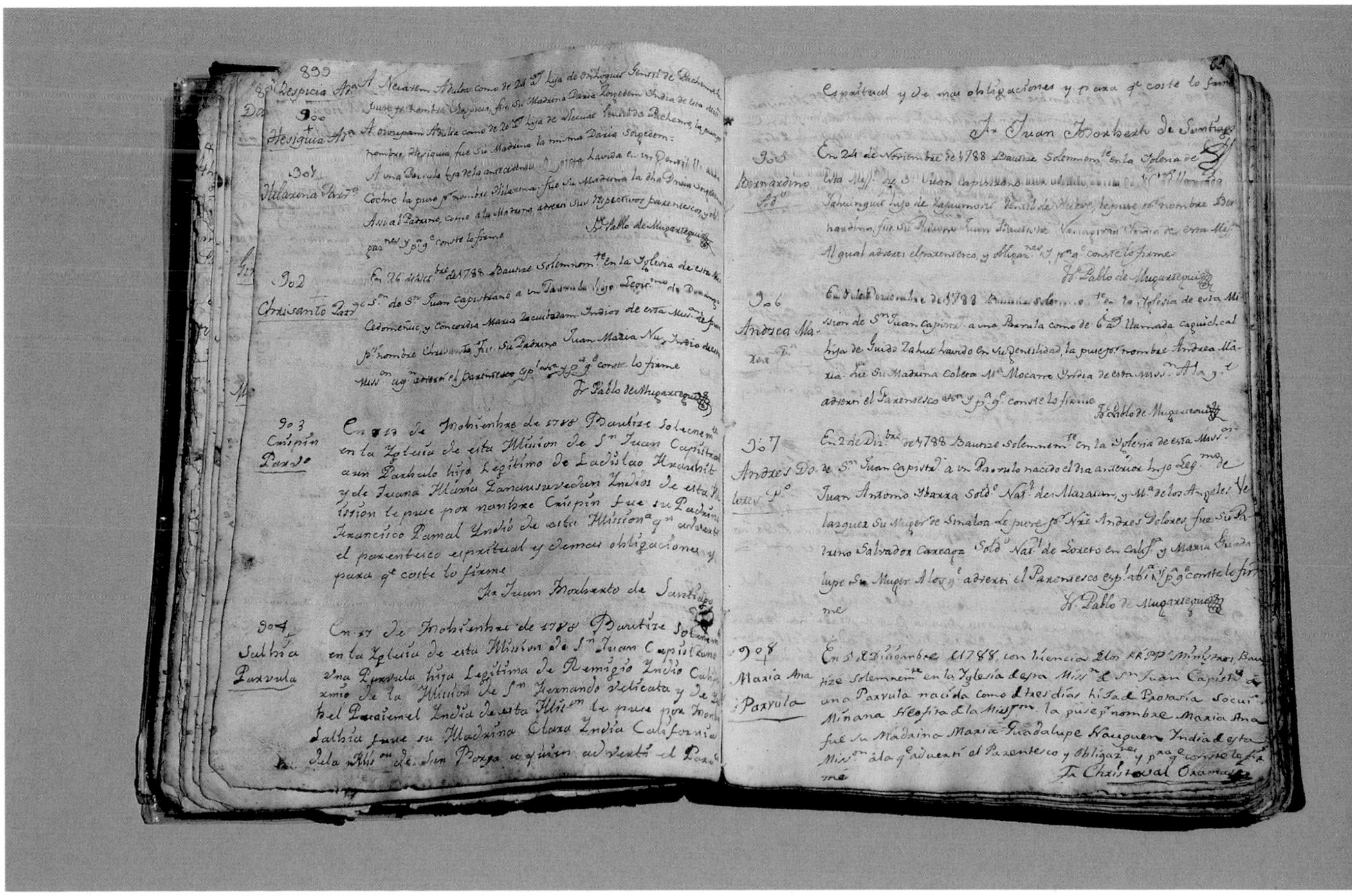

Spiritual Ministry Mission Registers

Year	Baptisms	Marriage	Burials	Year	Baptisms	Marriage	Burials
1776	4	0	0	1812	245	69	108
1777	40	6	3	1813	28	16	68
1778	120	29	4	1814	48	19	55
1779	70	21	4	1815	55	22	78
1780	54	15	11	1816	46	19	67
1781	61	9	20	1817	50	11	74
1782	49	11	25	1818	51	12	62
1783	47	10	14	1819	43	20	58
1784	111	25	18	1820	43	15	55
1785	113	37	17	1821	59	14	65
1786	64	22	24	1822	46	12	46
1787	79	28	25	1823	44	20	38
1788	100	27	36	1824	44	13	54
1789	85	21	25	1825	50	20	69
1790	62	20	68	1826	51	16	38
1791	38	9	41	1827	50	7	139
1792	88	29	31	1828	41	17	51
1793	228	51	54	1829	44	15	55
1794	66	22	55	1830	43	5	47
1795	75	6	50	1831	57	10	42
1796	95	28	84	1832	37	4	62
1797	127	26	46	1833	47	6	62
1798	67	17	64	1834	17	9	39
1799	72	16	83	1835	30	4	37
1800	94	16	115	1836	21	0	25
1801	77	27	61	1837	27	17	28
1802	61	23	55	1838	25	8	27
1803	98	25	85	1839	17	0	17
1804	86	28	84	1840	15	0	15
1805	332	91	32	1841	19	0	24
1806	76	26	213	1842	28	0	13
1807	103	22	58	1843	9	0	0
1808	72	6	68	1844	13	0	0
1809	61	11	52	1845	2	0	0
1810	64	14	40	1846	11	0	8
1811	126	23	130	1847	18	0	0

Chapel Holy Water Font

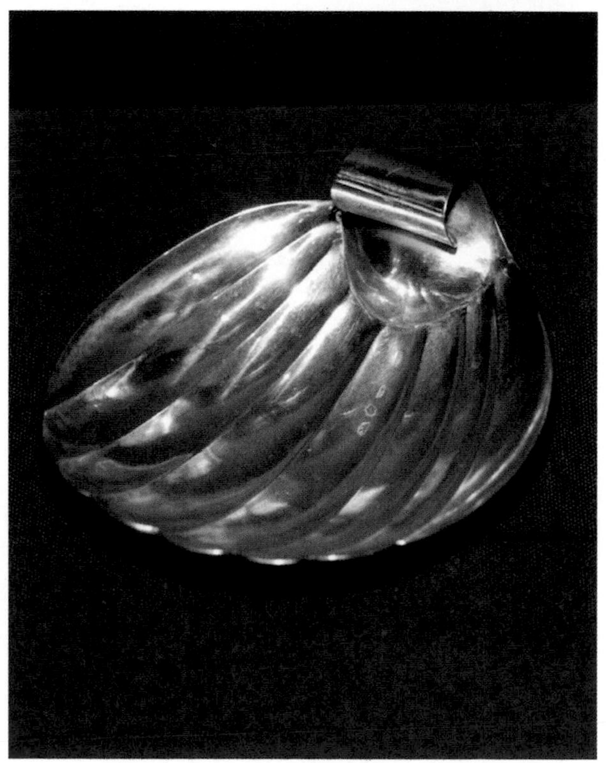

The Sacred Tradition continues

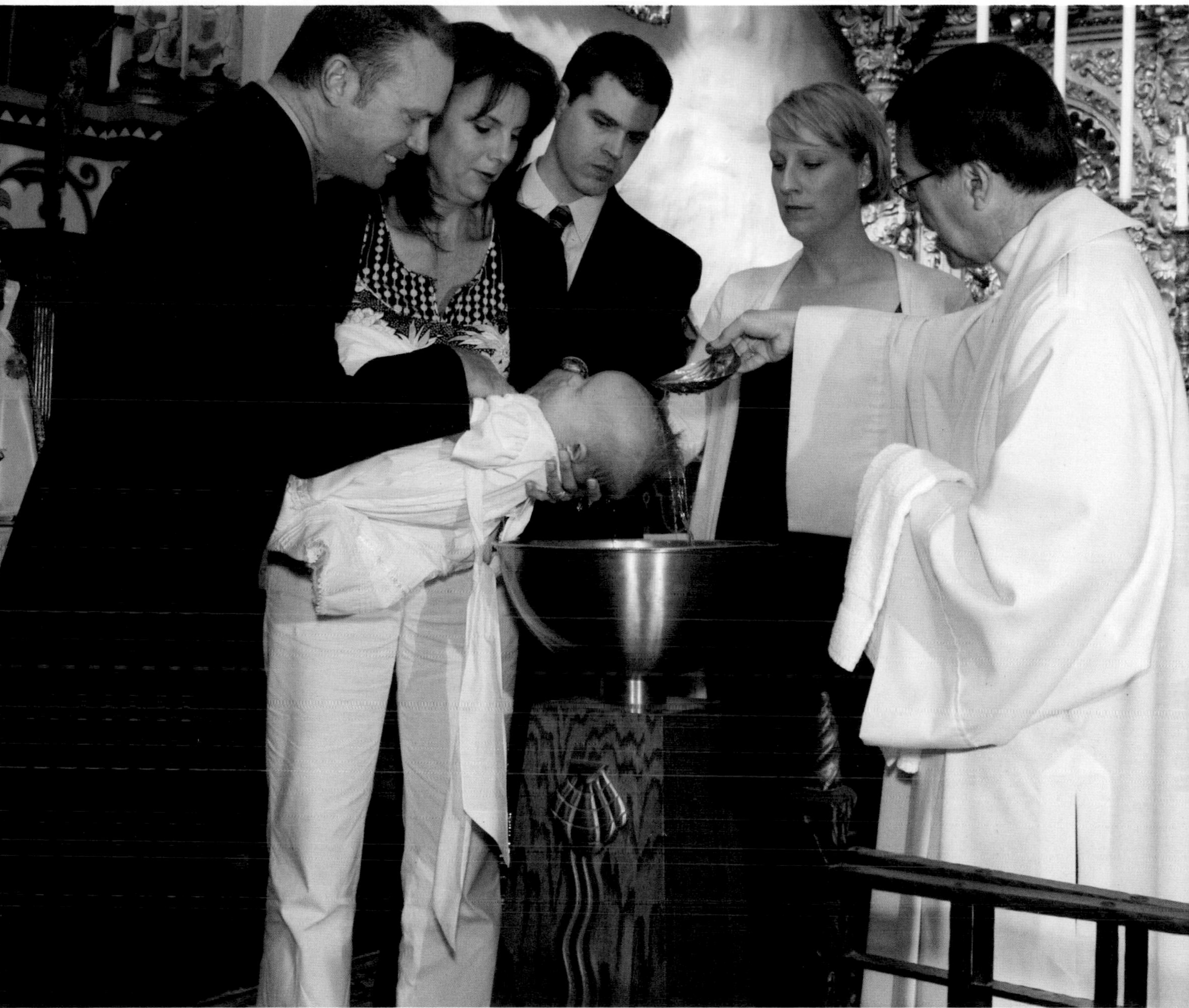

Rev. Monsignor Arthur A. Holquin, S.T.L., pastor of Mission Basilica San Juan Capistrano, baptizes Elena Grace Marchetti in the Serra Chapel

IN THIS HOLY PLACE LIE THE
BODIES OF THOSE WHO BUILT
THE MISSION · MAY THEIR SOULS
REST IN PEACE · ERECTED

Indian monument

IN THIS HOLY PLACE LIE THE
BODIES OF THOSE WHO BUILT
THE MISSION · MAY THEIR SOULS
REST IN PEACE · ERECTED 1924

THE RIGHT REV.
MSGR. ST. JOHN O'SULLIVAN
BORN MARCH 19, 1874
ORDAINED TO THE PRIESTHOOD
JUNE 12, 1904
DIED JULY 22, 1933
PASTOR OF OLD MISSION
1910—1933

JOSÉ ANTONIO YORBA I
BORN JULY 20, 1743
SAN SATURNINO, SPAIN
DIED JANUARY 16, 1825
RANCHO SANTA ANA, CALIFORNIA
MEMBER OF PORTOLÁ EXPEDITION 1769

› *Mission cemetery on the hill dates from about 1850s*

› *Charles Percy Austin*

VI The Great Stone Church

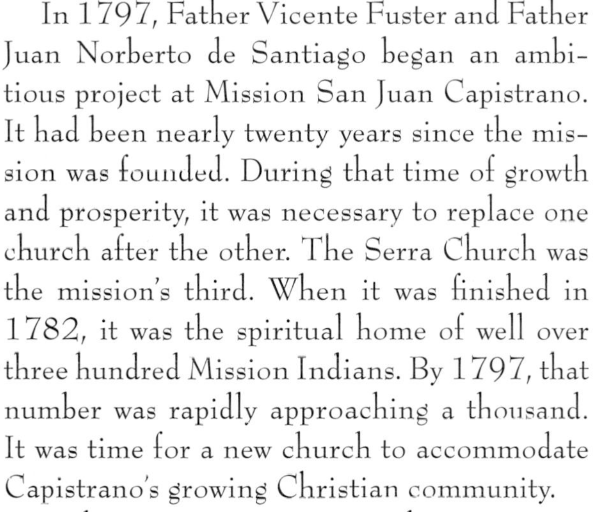

In 1797, Father Vicente Fuster and Father Juan Norberto de Santiago began an ambitious project at Mission San Juan Capistrano. It had been nearly twenty years since the mission was founded. During that time of growth and prosperity, it was necessary to replace one church after the other. The Serra Church was the mission's third. When it was finished in 1782, it was the spiritual home of well over three hundred Mission Indians. By 1797, that number was rapidly approaching a thousand. It was time for a new church to accommodate Capistrano's growing Christian community.

Father Fuster, age 55, arrived at Capistrano just a year after the mission was relocated to its present site. He served there for seventeen years and was responsible for much of its progress. Father Santiago, age 37, was the junior missionary, but already a veteran. By 1797, he had served alongside Father Fuster for nine years.

Together they had big plans for the mission's new church. It wasn't going to be just another, larger adobe church. It was going to be something special – something not yet seen in California. It was going to be a grand church made entirely of concrete and stone. It would compare well with the better churches back in "civilized" Mexico. Of course, it wasn't going to be easy. It would take a lot of time and hard work, but both these padres possessed the most important building resources: determination and perseverance. With that at hand, they laid the first stone for the church in a prayerful ceremony on March 2, 1797.

Material

The stone used in the church is limestone. There are two varieties: a yellow, fine-grained stone used for the walls and domes, and also a blue-grey stone used for the door and window jams and for the carefully carved interior details. This stone was taken from two principal locations. Much of it came from a site in the area of the Mision Vieja, about five or six miles east of the mission. This stone has been identified as a Santa Fe Tufa. Limestone was also brought up from the rocky area by the ocean known as San Juan Point.

Method

The work of bringing so much stone to the building site was a major effort and required many hands. Large stones were dragged in chains by oxen, then placed in oxcarts, or carretas, that took them to the mission. Local tradition recalls that long columns of Mission Indians – men, women, and even children – brought stone to the building site. Some carried the rocks in nets swung over their backs. Some carried them on litters and others just carried them by hand. It was regarded as a labor of love. Everyone wanted to be a part of building this new, beautiful house for God.

Construction

The padres had made the general plan. The Juaneños did most of the manual labor. Nevertheless, this major project required an experienced professional. The padres appealed to Governor José Joaquin Arrillaga to help them find one. He in turn wrote to Prudencio Ruiz de Equino in Los Alamos. Eventually, they secured the services of Isidro Aguilar from Culiacán. He arrived at the mission after a five-month journey. San Juan Capistrano finally had its expert stonemason.

Capistrano was like an ant-hill of activity – everyone busy with their appointed duties. Trenches were dug and filled with stones to serve as foundations. Two small buildings were taken down because they were in the way. Two new buildings were constructed to serve as shops and storage places. Lime was prepared and mortar mixed. Stones were sized, cut, and set into place. Gradually the walls began to rise from what had been a mere outline in the soil.

In 1800, the construction was moving along at a good pace. Some of the walls were in place and the vaulting of the roof was already underway. The main altar had arrived from Mexico and was considered an "elegant" piece "and very much to the liking of the missionaries."

This, sadly, was as much as Father Vicente Fuster would see of his beloved Great Stone Church. He had been suffering from a "chest ailment." In fact, Father José Faura, age 27, came to help out in March. On October 21, 1800, Father Fuster passed away at the mission he had served for nearly twenty-one years. He was fifty-eight years old. Father Santiago and Father Faura tended to him in his last hours. Since the Great Stone Church was not yet sufficiently ready, they interred his remains in the Serra Church. Father Santiago succeeded him as the senior missionary and Father Faura took on the junior role.

A month later, on November 22nd, an earthquake rumbled through the area. It caused serious cracks in the walls of the Great Stone Church and caused one of them to fall in one of the transepts. This halted the construction progress while extensive work had to be done to repair the damage. In hindsight, it seems as though this earthquake was a warning sign of thing to come.

Another ominous sign occurred three months later. On February 25, 1801, an earthquake damaged the neighboring Mission of San Gabriel. A new church was also being built there. It too had a concrete vaulted roof. When the earthquake hit, it cracked the roof, causing serious concerns that it might have to be taken down. Reluctant to undo all that previous work, they patched up the cracks and continued. Eventually, however, concern for safety prevailed. The concrete roof was removed and replaced by a roof of timber and tiles.

There was a major building setback at San Juan Capistrano in 1803. Isidro Aguilar, the master mason, passed away. There is no record of anyone replacing him. It seems likely that some other skilled person must have been found to continue the work. If not, perhaps, Aguilar had already accomplished enough that others, who helped him and learned from him, were able to finish the building.

Whatever the case may be, five of the concrete vaults were complete by the end of 1804. By the end of 1805, the vaults over the main structure were complete. And in 1806 the church structure was basically finished and ready for use.

Description

It had taken nine years to build, but when it was finished there was no finer church in California than the Great Stone Church of San

Juan Capistrano. It was cruciform, shaped like a Latin cross, with a long nave, sanctuary, and transepts, seven domes, a sacristy, and a bell tower. It was 180 feet long and 30 feet wide at the nave and 52 feet high. The transepts, east and west, were 19 feet and 21 feet long respectively. The sanctuary was paved with diamond shaped tiles and the floor of the nave was simply the bare earth. The walls varied in thickness from four to seven feet depending on their use and the structural load. A lantern made of square tiles, known as ladrillos, surmounted the large central dome. A bell tower at the southeastern corner was 25 feet square and rose to an estimated 80 feet. Above it, some old timers remembered a gilded cock. Some also claim that this tower could be seen out at sea and that the bells could be heard for miles. There was a baptistery in the first floor of the tower, and the bells hung in the upper three floors. A stone sacristy, 28 by 19 feet, was attached to the sanctuary on the northwestern side. It provided a place for vesting and for storage of liturgical items. The Great Stone Church surrounded by the rolling hills of the Capistrano Valley made for quite an impressive spectacle.

Alison S. Clark, Irvine Museum

Decorations

The main dome of the church has long since disappeared. Elderly residents related to Father O'Sullivan many years ago that there was a large red star on the inside center of this dome.

In spite of the destruction of the church, there remains in its ruins carved and painted decorations, reminders of its past, albeit primitive, glory. Some have seen in these decorations an Aztec influence, perhaps to the taste of the master mason from Culiacán.

Others feel they are mostly colorful plant and floral decorations suggesting growth and life. Such a theme has been found in the painted decorations of other California Missions. The surviving decorations in the dome of the chancel have been copied and placed in the same locations in the Mission Basilica Church.

Epidemic

At the beginning of 1806, an epidemic of measles broke out for the first time at San Juan Capistrano. This disease was unknown to the Indians who seemed to have had little or no immunity to it. It caused many deaths, both at the Mission and in outlying areas. Within the first two months of the year there were 133 deaths. By the end of the year the Mission's burial records listed 213. This blow to the community made the occasion of the church's completion bittersweet.

Dedication
September 7, 8, 9, 1806

In early California when there was a major celebration, it usually went on for days. After all, people had to travel a long distance and by slow means of transportation, so it was expected that their time and effort would be made worthwhile. Besides, hospitality was the hallmark of the times. So it was when, after so many years, it was time to dedicate the Great Stone Church of San Juan Capistrano.

Father José Faura wrote an account of the festivities in the mission's baptismal register:

"The baptism (of Lucas, an eight month old Indian) which precedes is the first which was administered in the new church of this Mission, constructed by the neophytes at the cost of supplication and labors. The whole is of masonry, lime, and stone, with vaulted roof of the same material and with a transept. It was commenced on the second day of February in the year 1797, the day dedicated to the Solemnity of the Purification of Mary Most Holy, and completed in the year 1806. It was blessed on the afternoon of September 7 of the said year by the Very Reverend Estevan Tápis, Preacher Apostolic of the College of San Fernando de Mexico, and Presidente of these Missions of New or Upper California, with the assistance of the Rev. Fathers José de Miguel and José Antonio de Urresti of the holy Province of Cantabria, missionaries Apostolic of the said College and missionaries of the neighboring Mission of San Gabriel Archangel; of the Rev. Father Marcos Antonio de Victoria, member of the same Province of Cantabria and of the said College and missionary of the Mission of Santa Barbara; of the Rev. Father José Zalvidea, member of the said Province and College, and missionary of the Mission of San Fernando Rey de España; of the Rev. Father Antonio Peyri, member of the holy Province of Catalonia and of the said College and missionary of the neighboring Mission of San Luis Rey de Francia; of the Rev. Father Pedro de la Cueva, member of the holy Province of Extremadura (infra Tagum), member of the said College, and ex-minister of the Mission of San José; of the Rev. Father Juan Norberto de Santiago, native of the pueblo of Samiano, contado de Trevino, in the Province of Alaba, member of the holy Province of Cantabria and member of said College; of the Rev. Father José Faura, native of Barcelona, Capital of the Principality of Catalonia, member of the holy Province of the same name and member of the said College.

"There assisted at the dedication also Don José Joaquín de Arrillaga, Lieutenant Colonel of the Royal Army and present Governor of this Province of Upper California; Don Miguel Rodriguez, Captain of the Cavalry Company and of the Presidio of San Diego; Don Francisco Maria Ruiz, Lieutenant of the Presidio Company of San Diego; Don Joaquín Maitorena, Ensign of the Company of the Presidio of Santa Barbara; and many individuals of said companies, many people called de Razon; many Neophytes of the near-by Missions and of others, besides all the Neophytes of this Mission.

"On the following day, September 8, Solemn High Mass was celebrated by the already mentioned Father Marcos Victoria, and the said Father Urresti preached.

"On the ninth of said month, the remains of the Rev. Father Vicente Fuster, late missionary of this Mission, were transferred from the old church to the new one; and after a Solemn High Mass of Requiem had been sung, which was celebrated by the said Father De la Cueva, and sermon on the Souls Departed preached by the said Faura, the said remains were deposited in a tomb which is in the presbytery on the Epistle side. At the function for the Souls Departed, besides the Fathers mentioned, were present the Rev. José Sanchez, member of the holy Province of Extremadura (supra Tagum) member of the said College and missionary of the Mission of San Diego, the first of all the Missions in Upper California; and Don Ignacio Martinez, Ensign of the Company of the Presidio of San Diego. In witness, whereof I sign this day, October 18, 1806, - Father José Faura."

Work in Progress

Although there were many interior improvements yet to be made, the most difficult work had been done and the new church was the pride of Capistrano. In this beautiful setting Masses, weddings, baptisms, funerals, and the great seasons and feasts of the liturgical year would be celebrated. Moreover, Capistrano now had a church that could comfortably accommodate its large congregation with room for still more. As time progressed there would be further opportunity for decorations and other enhancements.

Builders

The Juaneños built the Great Stone Church. Unfortunately, their names, in terms of who did what, have not come down to us in history. However, we can possibly identify some because of their known occupations. Ramon Benevenuto, born in 1781, was by trade a carpenter. It is likely that he was very much involved and, perhaps, even learned his trade on the job. In 1812 the padres gave him the honor of being the church sacristan.

Teofilo, also a Juaneño, was skilled as a painter. With the probable assistance of other Mission Indians, he was most likely responsible for the painted decorations in the new church – some of which have survived through the years.

Others who probably worked on the Stone Church were José Antonio Ramirez, a master carpenter and stonecutter, and Basilio Rosas, a mason. There were also government contract workers in California during this time and some of them are known to have been at San Juan Capistrano during the church's construction. They were Felipe Garcia Romero, a master blacksmith; Manuel Gutierrez, a carpenter; and Francisco Gomez, a master mason.

There were also two soldiers of the guard assigned to Capistrano who also had special construction skills. Manuel Vargas was a blacksmith and Carlos Rosas probably was trained in masonry by his father, already mentioned, Basilio Rosas. With these skilled men close at hand, it seems sure that they also worked on such an important project as the Great Stone Church.

Padres

Father José Faura had arrived at the Mission in 1800 when Father Fuster was very ill and soon to die. He participated in the dedication ceremonies of the Stone Church and preached at the Requiem Mass when Father Fuster's remains were interred in its sanctuary. He continued on at the Mission until 1809 when he departed for Mexico. He had completed his ten-year commitment to the California Missions.

Father Norberto de Santiago spent nearly twenty-two years at Capistrano. He had been there when the first stone had been laid for the new church. He saw it to its completion and participated in the dedication ceremonies. He served in it for the next four years until 1800 when he departed for Mexico. Both he and Father Faura were spared the shock and sorrow of an impending disaster.

Father Francisco Suñer arrived at San Juan Capistrano on March 4, 1810. Father Faura had already left and Father Santiago was preparing to leave. Father José Barona joined him at the Mission in April of the following year. Both padres were the same age, forty-six, but Father Barona was the more experienced missionary. Father Suñer was already forty when he first applied to become a missionary. Neither padre had been present at the dedication of the Great Stone Church, but both of them would share in its history in a way they couldn't have imagined, but would never forget.

Charles Percy Austin. Irvine Museum

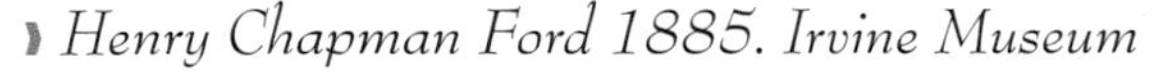

Henry Chapman Ford 1885. Irvine Museum

Disaster
The Earthquake of 1812

The story of the Great Stone Church is a sad story, even tragic. It's almost a metaphor for the Mission System itself, which collapsed under its own weight by forces unforeseen and uncontrollable.

It had taken nine years to build the Great Stone Church, but it was not destined to last even that long. In fact, it lasted just six years and three months to the day. On December 8, 1812, an earthquake shook Southern California and brought down most of the church. Worse yet, it killed at least forty Mission Indians. The missionaries reported the tragedy:

"On the eighth day of the month consecrated to the Most Pure Conception of the Most Holy Virgin, a terrible earthquake occurred while the first holy Mass was being celebrated in the morning. In a moment it completely destroyed the new church built of masonry. It required more than nine years to construct it, but it lasted no more than six years and three months to the day; for it was blessed on September 8, 1806. The tower tottered twice. At the second shock it fell on the portal and bore this down, causing the concrete roof to cave in as far as the transept exclusively. Forty Indians, thirty-eight adults and two children, were buried beneath the ruins, only six escaping as by a miracle. Of the whites, none were killed, though some were at the holy Mass. The worse of all is the death of those unfortunates. The mishap has left us without a church, for on account of clefts and breaks it is altogether unserviceable; and because the walls of the fallen part remain high, we dare not work and are in constant fear."

Fr. Francisco Suñer
Fr. José Barona

In the mission Death Register Father Barona writes the following statement and lists thirty-nine burials: "I gave ecclesiastical burial in the cemetery of the church of this Mission to the following male and female adults and to a child, who died buried beneath the ruins of the said church, which was destroyed on the eighth of said month and year at the time of the first holy Mass."

One can hardly imagine the terror that swept through the mission community as the earthquake struck. Those who frantically searched for survivors among the heavy ruins must have been stunned and shocked. There must have been heart-wrenching grief for those who searched the debris and discovered the crushed and lifeless bodies of their loved ones. Furthermore, their faith must have been sorely tested as they wondered how God could allow this, especially while their beloved were in church and at prayer. The padres, overcoming their own shock, had a lot of difficult consoling to do.

Among the thirty-nine first discovered, there were four married men, three single, twenty-five married women, four widows, two single women, and one male child. On February 26, 1813, more than two months later, workers clearing the site found the body of a woman, Paulina Quieran.

Two children who died in February may also have been victims of injuries in the disaster. Cirila, whose mother and twin brother had perished in the collapsed church, was buried on February 2nd. And Pantaleon Tomeanpuerinat, an eighteen-month old boy, was buried on February 13th.

Some of the old-timers recalled that there were two survivors pulled from the rubble. Two days after the quake, they heard someone groaning. They discovered a pregnant woman who had been spared in a little hollow made by the debris. Sometime later she became the happy mother of a new San Juaneño.

It was also remembered that the day of the earthquake was clear and unusually warm for December. It was a holy day, the Feast of the Immaculate Conception, and there were to be two Masses, an early Mass at about seven a.m. and a High Mass with a sermon at midmorning. It was during the first Mass, after the scripture readings, that the earthquake began. The first shock startled the people and then sent them scrambling for the doors. The padre, it is said, motioned for people to follow him as he exited through the sacristy door. Six other people also managed to make it out. A second more severe shock quickly followed and brought down the building. The bell tower crashed down at the front of the church. Some said it fell outwards towards the plaza. Others claimed it came down over the roof in front and brought down the concrete domes and walls on top of the victims. It seems the first shock warped the walls and caused the doors to jam. Most of the bodies were found crowded near the door on the west side.

The loss of life made this the greatest tragedy in all of California, but San Juan Capistrano was not the only mission damaged. The new church at San Gabriel was also badly cracked and the top of its bell tower collapsed. How far distant the earthquake was felt is not known. There is no record of damage at San Luis Rey or San Diego. Nevertheless, there was more to come.

Close-up of church ruins c. 1880s

Mission Ruins from a distance

The year 1812 has been called the "Año de los Temblores," the year of the earthquakes. Another earthquake, even more severe, struck on December 21st, causing wide damage. San Fernando suffered serious damage to its church. San Buenaventura had so much damage to its tower and façade that they had to be completely rebuilt. At Santa Barbara both the presidio and the mission were damaged. The church was so badly cracked that it was declared beyond repair. At Santa Inés all the roofs came down as well as the corner of the church. The worst damage occurred at La Purísima. The whole mission was so badly damaged that it had to be abandoned and completely relocated. Truly, the New Year, 1813, began with an agenda of repairs and restoration that no one had foreseen.

In spite of the earthquakes, an examination of the annual reports indicates that the first two decades of the 1800s was a time of general prosperity. The missions were well organized and became more efficient and productive. Yet, almost unnoticed, events were brewing in Mexico that would have dire consequences. The Mexican revolution against Spain was just beginning.

Observations

Several early, prominent visitors to Mission San Juan Capistrano and its Great Stone Church were very much impressed with the church, even in its ruins. They have provided us with their recollections.

In 1829, California pioneer and author, Alfred Robinson, had this to say: "There remain (at Capistrano) the ruins of an immense church, which was destroyed by an earthquake in 1812, when many Indians were buried in its fall. It still bears the appearance of having been one of the best-finished structures of the country, and the workmanship displayed in the sculpture upon its walls and its vaulted roof would command admiration in our own country."

On January 5, 1847, Commodore Robert Stockton, U.S.N. visited San Juan Capistrano and observed that the Great Stone Church was "evidently once a handsome building; well-finished with cut stone arches over doors, windows, etc.; the cornice of the same; the rest of the building of stone, covered with cement and stucco work."

Major William H. Emory, U.S.A. gave his impression, also in 1847: "The cathedral was once a fine strong building, with an arched cupola; only one-half of the building , capped by a segment of the cupola, is now standing, the other part having been thrown down by an earthquake in the year 1812, killing some thirty or forty persons who had fled to it for refuge."

› *Groundbreaking: January 31, 1982*

POWER
FOR
RENT

Our Lady of Guadalupe

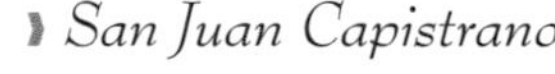

San Juan Capistrano

SAN
RAſAEL
ARCANGEL
ORA
PRO
NOBIS

Saint Peregrine

"O Lord, I love the house where You dwell, the place where your Glory abides" (Psalm 26)

Gary M. Tinnes, Troy A. Tertany

VII Mission as Rancho

"You make the grass grow for the cattle and the plants to serve man's needs, that he may bring forth bread from the earth and wine to cheer man's heart; oil to make him glad and bread to strengthen man's heart."
(Psalm 104)

The purpose of the Mission was to convert the Indians to Christianity and to teach them the skills they would need to survive in a modern civilization. In order to accomplish this, it was thought best that the Mission Indians should live in a community at the Mission. Of course, the physical needs of the community would have to be provided – people had to be sheltered, fed, and clothed. In the beginning, the supplies brought up from Mexico would get the Mission started, but this would be just for the first years. After that, the Mission would need to be self-supporting. The Mission would train the Indians in the skills needed to run a great, communal rancho with livestock and agricultural produce providing food and other necessities.

Livestock

The Indians had not seen the kinds of animals that the Spaniards had brought to their world in 1769. Horses, cattle, and mules were a wonder to them. However, by 1776 when San Juan Capistrano was founded, they were accustomed to seeing them. And these animals would become a very important part of their lives.

Variety

In 1783 the missions were required to make a detailed report on both their spiritual and material progress. Reports on the livestock included cattle, sheep, goats, pigs, horses, and mules. This was thought sufficient, but did not include all the creatures common to the missions. There were also chickens, doves, ducks, geese, and turkeys. As early as 1780, a chicken coop and dove cot were built at the Mission.

Hunters also brought in rabbits, deer, and even bear. Indian fishermen would also add their catches to the menu. The Mission had animals for work, transportation, and a wide variety of ingredients for the communal stew, the pazole.

Cattle

In 1776 San Juan Capistrano started with eighty-three head of cattle. Father Serra himself brought them down from San Gabriel. In 1783, when the first report was made, there were already 430. Three years later, it was over a thousand. In 1819, the missionaries reported an amazing 16,000 head of cattle!

In the early years, the missions were discouraged from killing cattle, except in dire necessity. The herd had to be left alone in order to increase. That increase was to be shared with new missions just starting out. Fortunately, the cattle cooperated and prospered quite well in California.

Origins

The cattle introduced into California were Mexican – brought up from Baja and Sonora. They were the descendents of the original stock brought over from Spain by Cortés in the 16th Century. They were strong, agile, and considered large by the standards of the day. A good steer might weigh as much as 600 to 800 pounds. Contemporary writers described them as having long, curving horns and sloping hindquarters. Some were black and others a reddish brown. Many had a white stripe down their back. These were known as "Line Backs." Mission cattle were a hearty breed and well suited to the landscape.

Vaqueros

The missions would not have succeeded without the cattle and those who were trained to take care of them – the vaqueros, or cowboys. In the beginning, when the herd was small, the cattle were kept close to the Mission. During this time an experienced soldier of the guard, or a Christian Indian from Baja, would teach Mission Indians the skills of the vaquero. A vaquero had to be an expert horseman and roper.

At first the government objected to Indians learning to ride horses. They feared they would become like the Apaches of the Sonora who learned to ride horses and raided and harassed Spanish settlements. The missionaries argued, successfully, that they absolutely needed vaqueros and the Mission Indians were the only ones available to do this work. The government reluctantly yielded to the logic of the argument.

Pastures

A corral was one of the first things built at the new mission site in 1778. A wooden calf barn was erected the next year. Two years later a corral, 138 feet square was built on the west side of the mission. An adobe calf barn 8 by 22 feet replaced the wooden barn in 1782. An adobe cattle corral about 165 feet square was built in 1783. Within this was a bullpen about 55 by 33 feet in size. A new corral, partly of adobe and partly of palisades, was constructed in 1786. Another corral 165 feet square was built in 1789. Yet another corral, 165 feet square was added in 1793.

As the herds increased in number, it was necessary to find larger pastures for them and good sources of water. Capistrano was situated between Missions San Gabriel and San Luis Rey. Within this territory the vaqueros divided up the cattle according to the size of the various places where animals could graze. Some of these were far enough away from the Mission proper that adobe haciendas were provided for the vaqueros to live there. These sites were known as estancias. One of these, southwest of the Mission, was known as Rancho San Mateo. Another was located on the Plano Trabuco (now the City of Santa Margarita). There were also pasturages in the Saddleback Valley and along the Santa Ana River. An estancia preserved in Costa Mesa marks one of these grazing locations. Of course, some cattle were always kept at the Mission itself. Milk cows provided the Mission's much needed milk, butter, and cheese. In 1782 a quesero (cheese factory) was built at the north end of the Mission's west wing.

Ranching

Working under a foreman called a mayordomo, the vaqueros had many duties. They had to keep the herd together, round up the strays, and move them to good grazing sites and water. Together with their dogs, they also had to protect the cattle from predators: coyotes, mountain lions, bears, and Indian rustlers.

In the late summer or early fall, the vaqueros held their annual rodeo, or round up. Sometimes branded cattle from another mission or private owner would get mixed in and would have to be separated out. They would also have to brand and earmark the calves. They also counted the cattle to prepare for the Mission's annual report.

From the beginning every Mission and every cattle owner had to register with the government a brand and an identifying earmark, or señal. In the early days a brand would be designed for each mission and a corresponding branding iron, or fierro, would be produced and sent up from Mexico. Later these were made in the mission's own blacksmith shop. The brand for Mission San Juan Capistrano was easily recognized. It was simply "CAP."

Vaqueros also selected cattle for oxen. They broke them to the yoke which was tied to their horns. They trained them to pull plows and carts called carretas. It was heavy work suitable to the strength of these powerful bovines.

Courtesy Dr. Edward H. and Yvonne Boseker

Matanzas

Vaqueros also carried out the matanzas. This was not a pretty job, but a very important one. They selected cattle from the herd to be slaughtered. This was done on a weekly basis and provided food for the community. They roped a steer, brought it down, killed, skinned, and butchered it. They cut away the lean meat which was hauled away on carretas to the Mission kitchen. Some of the meat was consumed right away and some was dried or "jerked" for later consumption. Fats were also cut away and taken to the mission for processing and storing as tallow. Tallow was made into candles and the lighter fats were made into soap. Both of these items were of everyday importance.

When it is remembered that the Mission Indian population at San Juan Capistrano increased to over a thousand, it shouldn't be surprising that fifty head of cattle – or more if needed – were slaughtered for food during the weekly matanzas. Beef became a regular, expected, and desirable part of the Mission Indian diet.

Later, when the herds became very large, it was necessary to thin them out to preserve the limited pastureland. A major matanza was held about May of each year. Sometimes hundreds of cattle were slaughtered in a period lasting as long as three months. Hides and tallow were collected and stored at the Mission. What wasn't used at the Mission became an important commodity that could be sold or traded for other goods. Of course, the major matanzas caused a lot of waste. There was much more meat than could be used at the Mission. Sometimes the carcasses were burned and other times they were just left to the appetites of the birds and wild animals.

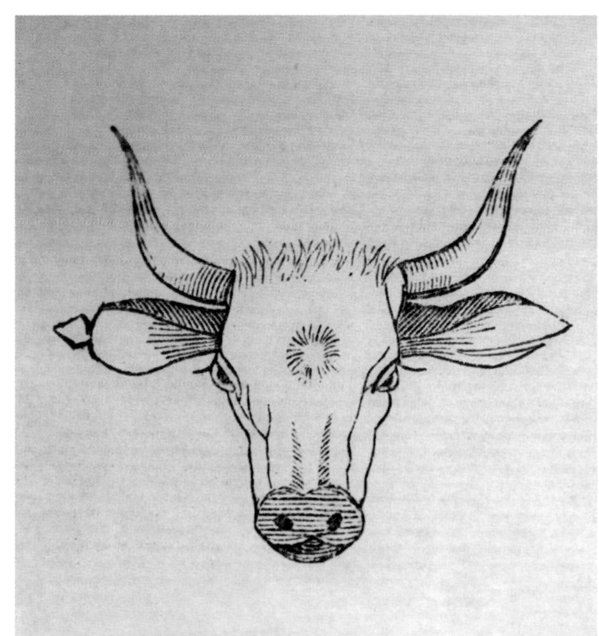

Tannery

Between 1790 and 1795 two tanners and two saddle makers came from Mexico to California. They taught their skills to the Mission Indians who, in turn, taught them to others. The extensive remains of San Juan Capistrano's tannery works were uncovered in the 1930s and may be seen behind the west wing of the Mission's quadrangle.

Hides were turned into leather at the Mission tannery. They were soaked for several days in a heavy lime solution. Hair and bits of flesh and fat were then carefully scraped off. The bare hides were then washed and washed again. Afterwards, they were placed in a large tanning vat or tank. A layer of crushed oak bark was spread out over the bottom of the vat. A hide was placed on top of it and another layer of crushed oak bark placed on top of it. In this manner the hides were stacked up like oak bark sandwiches. Water was poured over this stack of hides and left to soak for three or more months. Occasionally, they would be removed and repacked in the same way. When they were finally removed, they were washed clean again. Then the Indian workers rubbed them with oil or tallow to make them soft and flexible. Following this they were placed in well-ventilated drying rooms. Although this was a long, tedious process, leather was a very useful commodity and worth the effort.

Mission

brand

Round up at Rancho Mission Viejo

Leather Products

Skilled Mission Indians turned leather into many different items. Saddle makers manufactured riding saddles for horses and mules. They made carriers for the pack animals, bridle-reins, and whips. Leatherworkers cut leather and braided it into strong ropes called reatas or lassos. They also made such useful things as sacks, buckets, hinges, door covers, and ties that bound together beams in construction instead of nails. They even made them strong enough to hang the mission bells. Shoemakers provided boots, shoes, and belts. The art of tanning and working leather was an important skill for "civilized" life on the frontier.

Untanned hides were also put to use. When taken from the animal they were cured with salt, stretched out, and pegged to the ground. Later, although they quite stiff, they were cut and used for the bottoms of beds, chairs, and as mats for the bottom of the carretas.

Trade

Annual supply ships provided much needed goods for the California Missions. However, this service came to an end when the Mexican Revolution began in 1810. When this happened the missions had to supply food and goods not only for the Mission Indians, but also for the California Military and others.

Initially the government forbade trade with foreign vessels, but this eventually became a necessity. There was no other way to receive products they could not make themselves. Local authorities became content to allow the traffic, providing they could, of course, collect tariffs on the imported goods. After 1816, foreign trading ships regularly plied the coastal waters. They had a good market at home for hides and tallow and other California products. California did not have cash money to buy needed hardware and general merchandise. The trading ships served as general stores and were often set up like them. Mission products could be traded for metals, gun powder, guns, furniture, religious goods, bolts of various kinds of cloth, ribbons, beads, barrels, plow points, hoes, shovels, knives, utensils, tableware, and a wide variety of desirable products, not the least of which was the padres' personal favorite – chocolate! Everyone looked forward to the coming of the trading ships. This became so important that Indian labor and mission products soon became the basis of the California economy, especially after Mexico's independence from Spain in 1822.

Richard Henry Dana
Two years before the mast
1836

"We all went on shore in the quarter-boat, with the long boat (filled with goods) in tow. As we drew in, we descried an ox-cart and a couple of men standing directly on the brow of the hill (Dana Point); and having landed; the captain took his way around the hill, ordering me and one other to follow him. We followed, picking our way out, and jumping and scrambling up, walking over briars and prickly pears, until we came to the top. Here the country stretched out for miles, as far as the eye could reach, on a level, table surface, and the only habitation in sight was the small white mission of San Juan Capistrano, with a few Indian huts about it, standing in a small hollow, about a mile from where we were. Reaching the brow of the hill, where the cart stood, we found several piles of hides, and Indians sitting around them. One or two of the carts were coming slowly on from the Mission, and the captain told us to begin and throw the hides down. This, then, was the way they were to be got down – thrown down, one at a time, a distance of four hundred (280) feet! This was doing business on a great scale. Standing on the edge of the hill, and looking down the perpendicular height, the sailors that walked upon the beach appeared like mice; and our tall anchoring bark diminished to her cock; her cock a buoy almost too small for sight.

Down this height we pitched the hides, throwing them as far out into the air as we could; and as they were large and stiff, and doubled, like the cover of a book, the wind took them, and they swayed and eddied about, plunging and rising in the air, like a kite when it has broken its string. As it was now low tide, there was no danger of their falling into the water; and as fast as they came to the ground, the men below picked them up, and taking them on their heads, walked off with them to the boat. It was really a picturesque sight; the great height, the scaling of the hides, and the continual walking to and fro of the men, who looked like mites on the beach. This was to romance of hide droghing!

(Two Years Before the Mast, Richard Henry Dana, New York, 1840)

Dana Point

The Pilgrim

Horses

Horses were needed for riding. They were the principal means of transportation. Californios became famous for their riding skills. Horses and their riders worked as an expert team in roping cattle. Every good vaquero had to be a good caballero.

California horses were the descendants of the horses Cortés brought over from Spain in 1517. They were small, but fast and possessed remarkable endurance. The military and vaqueros used them strictly for riding. Hauling and any other such work were left to the oxen.

Vaqueros kept the horses together, protected them from predators, and led them to good pasturage. They branded them to mark mission ownership and, in due time, broke them to the reins, the saddle, and the rider.

When San Juan Capistrano was founded in 1776, there were not even enough horses for the soldiers of the guard. In 1783, the missionaries counted 32 in their annual report. Ten years later, it was up to nearly 400. In 1806, it reached its highest count of 1,408. Horses were shared with other missions as needed. Not all the horses were fit for riding. Sometimes, if the herd became too large and there was insufficient pasturage, there would be a matanza to cut back on the numbers. Whatever hides and tallow could be obtained were taken to the mission tanning and tallow works.

Mules

A mule is the offspring of a female horse, a mare, and a male donkey, or burro. Mules don't reproduce themselves and, although much needed, were scarce on the frontier of Alta California. The first ones were brought up in the first land expeditions to San Diego from Baja in 1769.

Mules were the principal beast of burden. They were the pack animals that carried goods and equipment from one place to another. They could go where the cumbersome ox carts could not go. They made possible the very beginning of the California Missions in 1769. They brought the necessary provisions for various other exploration parties. Sometimes, especially in the early years, the decision as to whether or not new missions could be established depended on the sufficient availability of mules. Pack mules carried essential goods from one mission to another. They carried goods to and from the trading ships. Mules and the muleteers, who packed them and tended to them, were an important component of California's mission and colonization program.

Mules were also used for riding. They were the especially preferred means of transportation for the Franciscan Padres. This was their tradition and was considered more in keeping with the humble state of life to which they had committed themselves. Of course, walking barefoot was considered even more exemplary, but that was not practical for long distances and rough country.

At San Juan Capistrano there were just 11 mules in 1783. Ten years later there were 36. They topped 100 in 1808 and reached the highest number, 183, in 1813.

The mission also had donkeys. These smaller animals were used primarily for breeding mules and for supplying the muscle power in turning heavy millstones.

Pigs

Unlike the large animals, pigs could be easily brought up on the supply ships from Mexico. Every mission started off with a few. They were used, of course, for food. Smoked hams and other pork products were a tasty part of the mission menu.

In 1783, there were 40 pigs counted in the pens at Capistrano. The number was never very large, probably because of their consumption. Nevertheless, they reported 206 pigs – their highest count – in 1818.

Sheep

The first sheep in Alta California were brought overland from Baja to Mission San Diego in 1772. No other mission had them until 1777. That year San Diego reimbursed San Juan Capistrano for aid it had received with a payment that included ten sheep and eleven goats. By 1783, Capistrano had a flock of 305 sheep. That year a sheep corral, about138 feet-square, was built. It had smaller pens for lambs and ewes. Ten years later, the sheep count was an amazing 8,820. And seven years later, in 1800, it reached its highest count ever at an even more amazing 17,030 sheep! Although that number declined, it remained in the thousands until the end of the mission period.

Shepherds, called pastores, guarded the sheep and pastured them. They branded, sheared, and even slaughtered them when necessary. With such large flocks, the shepherd's work was both a busy and important part of mission life.

Sheep were a great resource, providing food and clothing for the community. Mutton was a change of fare from the abundant beef that had become so much a part of the mission diet. When these animals were slaughtered for food, their skins went to the tannery and their fat went to the tallow works. Even so, it was the live sheep that produced the most important commodity for the mission: wool. From this the Mission Indians learned to make blankets, shirts, breeches, and even hats.

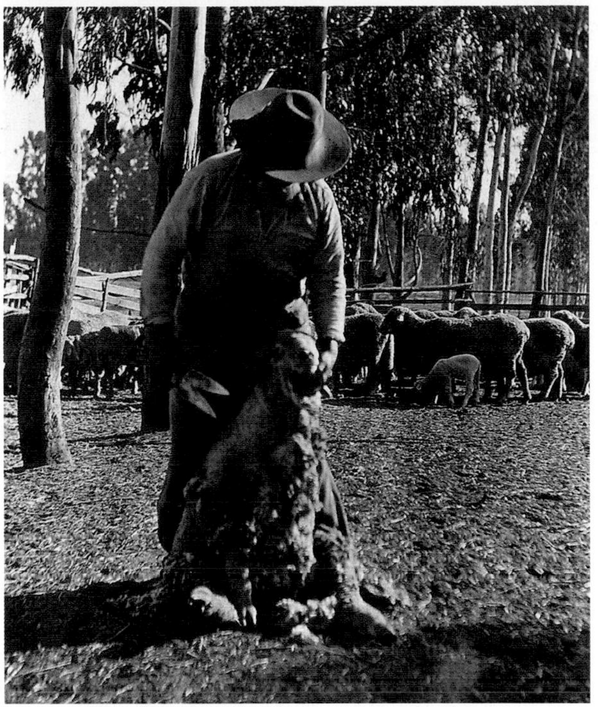

Of course, professionals were required to teach these skills. Wool had to be sheared and cleaned. It was then carded, straightened, and spun into thread. This thread was placed on a loom and made into cloth. The cloth was then dyed, dried, and cut for sewing into various items of clothing.

In the early 1790s a weaving instructor, Antonio Domingo Henríquez, visited all the missions from San Diego to San Luis Obispo. He and his Indian wife taught the rudiments of carding, spinning, and weaving. He also made the necessary equipment: spinning wheels, warping frames, looms, and combs.

In 1796, the padres directed the building of a spinning room. It was forty-four by seventeen feet in dimensions and had a brick floor. It was put to use immediately because that summer the government sent another professional weaver, Mariano Mendoza, and his wife to provide further training to the Juaneños. Together they wove baize, woolen blankets, cloth of mixed cotton and wool, thirty yards of white flannel, and a carpet for the church. They also sent 2,600 pounds of white wool and 500 pounds of black wool to the Presidio of Monterey. The Mission Indians and their shops were becoming very productive.

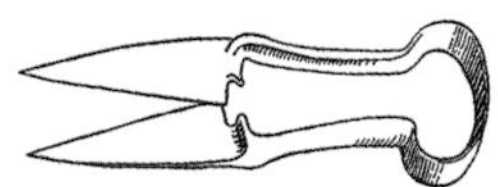

Goats

Goats provided milk, cheese, and occasionally mutton for the mission table. In 1777, San Juan Capistrano received eleven goats from Mission San Diego. In 1784, they had 1,353! That was highest number ever. Usually the goat herd was in the more manageable lower hundreds – still a significant part of the mission livestock.

Tallow Works

At the matanzas the butchers would cut out the animal fat as well as the meat. They did this whenever animals were slaughtered whether they were cattle, horses, sheep, goats, or pigs. At the Mission the Indian workers divided the hard fat from the rest. This fat, taken from the loins and around the kidneys, is called sebo de rama, or suet. It was placed in a cauldron or tallow vat with water. This mixture was heated until the water evaporated and the suet was rendered, or melted. While the liquid fat was still warm, water was again added. After this mixture cooled, the rendered fat rose to the top as tallow. When this was removed and dried out, it was placed in bags made of hides and stored in a cool area. It was probably in 1792 that the tallow rendering works and dyeing vats were constructed.

The Bat Boy of San Juan

In March of 1801, a young Indian boy entered into a darkened mission warehouse to get some tallow. He was carrying a candle to light his way. He was distracted by some bats and tried to kill them. In the process he accidentally set the whole place on fire. He was spared – to await later chastisement – but the fire destroyed 12,500 pounds of tallow and a thousand bushels of corn and wheat. The building was so badly damaged that it had to be rebuilt the following year. The young man achieved a remarkable, though unwanted, notoriety.

Candle Works

Candles were made from tallow. This was usually done in cool weather. The tallow was heated until it was lukewarm. Wick strings suspended from sticks were dipped into the tallow, pulled out to cool a bit, and then dipped again. This was repeated until the candle was of the desired thickness. Later, when candle molds became available, the warm tallow was simply poured into them and allowed to cool. Hundreds of candles were used at the Mission. Extra candles were made available for trade.

Soap Works

Soap was made from combining fat and ashes. Ashes were removed from mission furnaces and leached in hot water. Tallow rendered from the lighter, greasier scrap fats was melted and added into this alkaline solution. This was boiled for a time until gradually soap rose to the top. It was skimmed off and placed into a mold. When sufficiently dry, bars were cut and placed on shelves until they were thoroughly dry and ready for use. Surplus soap was used for trade.

Remnants of a mission furnace

Livestock

Year	Cattle	Horses	Mules	Sheep	Goats	Pigs	Total
1783	430	32	11	305	830	40	1,648
1784	703	50	12	904	1,353	20	3,042
1785	866	50	12	1,300	850	30	3,108
1786	1,109	63	14	1,855	869	29	3,939
1787	1,300	68	39	2,440	990	25	4,862
1788	1,360	80	22	2,507	808	30	4,807
1789	-	-	-	-	-	-	-
1790	2,328	176	22	4,700	808	-	8,034
1791	2,490	218	30	6,301	1,090	-	10,129
1792	3,451	246	28	8,206	608	-	12,539
1793	3,560	389	36	8,820	390	-	13,195
1794	3,500	441	44	9,114	458	-	13,557
1795	4,180	450	38	11,130	420	-	16,218
1796	4,720	532	58	12,050	150	-	17,510
1797	5,550	690	59	12,850	-	-	19,149
1798	7,256	484	68	13,748	-	-	21,556
1799	7,514	582	46	16,850	-	-	24,992
1800	7,815	567	50	17,030	-	-	25,462
1801	8,864	638	58	16,300	-	-	25,860
1802	8,710	660	58	15,300	-	-	24,728
1803	9,124	790	58	15,345	-	-	25,317
1804	10,316	908	70	15,520	-	-	26,814
1805	-	-	-	-	-	-	-
1806	11,228	1,408	92	12,350	-	-	25,078
1807	11,310	804	96	12,800	-	-	25,010
1808	10,850	836	113	14,200	-	-	25,999
1809	9,680	708	96	13,200	-	-	23,684
1810	9,200	538	100	11,500	-	-	21,338
1811	9,900	302	135	12,000	-	60	22,397
1812	10,300	380	171	12,500	-	50	23,401
1813	10,308	346	183	12,000	-	80	22,917
1814	10,000	370	160	10,200	60	40	20,830
1815	12,000	370	163	13,000	60	110	25,703
1816	12,500	438	163	14,000	75	160	27,336
1817	13,200	663	166	15,300	195	200	29,724
1818	13,000	689	157	15,800	237	206	30,089
1819	14,000	740	126	16,000	215	182	31,263
1820	11,000	381	99	13,800	203	195	25,678
1821	12,000	608	115	13,000	94	200	26,017
1822	11,500	531	112	12,000	83	145	24,371
1823	11,000	437	95	10,800	35	94	22,461
1824	-	-	-	-	-	-	-
1825	-	-	-	-	-	-	-
1826	10,800	345	51	5,700	55	40	16,991
1827	12,600	386	60	6,200	60	50	19,356
1828	9,600	293	28	5,600	52	63	15,636
1829	9,200	241	30	5,200	41	70	14,782
1830	-	-	-	-	-	-	-
1831	10,900	290	30	4,800	50	40	16,110
1832	-	-	-	-	-	-	-
1833	-	-	-	-	-	-	-
1834	8,000	50	9	4,000	-	80	12,139

Indian Diet

In their pre-mission days the local Indians had an interesting and colorful diet by comparison to what was considered "civilized" standards. Their regular fare consisted of seeds and acorns, roasted and ground into a meal. Berries and wild vegetable roots added taste to the cuisine. These items were painstakingly gathered and prepared by the women. The men added to the menu by hunting deer, rabbits, coyotes, squirrels, owls, and hawks. Occasionally they would bring in a catch of fish. And besides this delicious fare, the Indian palate was not at all adverse to such delicacies as rats, skunks, frogs, snails, worms, lizards, snakes, grasshoppers, crickets, and caterpillars. Even after the Spaniards introduced them to common European food, they also continued to enjoy the traditional food of their ancestors, usually at home in their Indian huts.

Agriculture

"They sow fields and plant their vines;
these yield crops for the harvest.
He blesses them; they grow in numbers.
He does not let their herds decrease."
(Ps.107)

The missionaries taught the Indians how to cultivate the earth and grow large quantities of agricultural products to provide a steady supply of food for their immediate and future needs. Although this food was different, they liked it and were happy not to have to go in search for it.

The Spanish government required the missionaries to report each year on the progress of their agricultural production. The missions were expected to achieve self-sufficiency in food within five years. The report was limited to eight classes of food: wheat, barley, corn, beans, peas, lentils, garbanzos (chickpeas), and habas (lima beans). These were important crops and served as a measure of their growing independence and prosperity, but the variety of food produced at the missions was far greater than just these items.

Wheat, corn, and barley were staple food sources at the missions. They required good land and a dependable water supply. Areas chosen for new mission sites were selected with this in mind. Each mission started off with seeds for these crops and usually had – besides the padres – Christian Indians from Baja, or borrowed from another mission, to help teach the art of cultivation. Such was the case at Capistrano.

Farming

Mission Indians had to be taught farming. Land had to be selected, cleared, and plowed. Indians had to learn how to plow with an ox team. Seed had to be scattered and covered. The field needed to be watered, weeded, and protected from birds and anything or anyone that might disturb the planting.

At harvest time the crops had to be cut with sickle and scythe. Wheat grains were separated from the tops of the grass. The rest was straw used for fodder, animal bedding, brick making, and roof thatching. The wheat grains were collected and threshed. Seeds were separated from their husks by trampling or beating them. The wheat kernels were separated from the chaff by winnowing – throwing the mixture into the air so that the breeze would blow away the lighter chaff.

Indian women placed the grain into stone containers called metates and crushed it with hand held stones called manos. They were familiar with this work because that is the way they processed the wild seeds they had gathered in their pre-mission days. By crushing grain in this way they produced flour that could be used to make bread, tortillas, or used as a meal mixed in with their common gruel, atole and pazole.

Wheat, Corn, and Barley

In 1783, the first year of the annual reports, San Juan Capistrano produced 833 bushels of wheat and 1,333 bushels of corn. Ten years later, it produced 5,840 bushels of wheat and 1, 867 bushels of corn. The highest amount of wheat was harvested in 1818 when they counted 8,616 bushels. However, the numbers decreased dramatically after that. The highest amount of corn produced was in 1806 with a harvest of 3,858 bushels. The major decline in corn did not start until 1828.

Barley was not a major crop at Capistrano. None was reported until 1791 and then it was just 87 bushels. It did have one banner year, 1811, when it went up to 3,167 bushels, but it dropped to 333 bushels the following year. In many years there was no barley production at all.

The other reported crops were beans, peas, lentils, garbanzos (chickpeas), and habas (lima beans). None of these even came close to the grains in production. Beans amounted to 66 bushels in 1783. Ten years later there were 292 bushels. The highest on record for Capistrano was 343 bushels in 1811, but the following year it was down to just 9 bushels. The highest number of peas grown was 50 bushels in 1828. Lentils were seldom grown, but the mission reported a high of 18 bushels in 1800. Garbanzos reached a high of 32 bushels in 1813, but there was none the following year. Habas (lima beans) were not planted until 1801 when they harvested 12 bushels. It went up to a high of 117 bushels in 1819, but declined rapidly after that.

Counting all the mission crops together, in 1783 Mission San Juan Capistrano produced 2,700 bushels. In 1811, a remarkably productive year, it peaked at an impressive 15,272 bushels.

Crop production generally increased with the years. As time went on there were more mouths to feed, but more hands to do the labor. Of course, productivity also depended on rainfall. Both drought and politics were bad for plants and animals. The numbers decreased in times of drought which were as unpredictable as they were unmerciful. The same could be said of politics. Food production decreased dramatically after Mexican Independence and Mission Secularization. In 1834 the padres were only able to report 283 bushels of agricultural products for the whole year.

Agricultural production (In Bushels)

Year	Wheat	Corn	Beans	Barley	*Other	Total
1783	833	1,333	67	-	-	2,233
1784	667	2,383	100	-	-	3,150
1785	1,345	1,500	217	-	-	3,062
1786	893	1,727	217	-	-	2,837
1787	1,500	1,167	250	-	7	2,924
1788	1,750	1,167	117	-	7	3,041
1789	-	-	-	-	-	-
1790	1,700	1,717	45	-	-	3,462
1791	2,643	3,090	227	87	-	6,046
1792	4,725	3,333	83	100	-	8,241
1793	5,840	1,867	292	-	-	7,999
1794	4,150	1,628	117	-	-	5,895
1795	4,100	1,583	175	-	-	5,858
1796	5,295	1,847	23	-	12	7,177
1797	4,670	478	125	-	-	5,273
1798	3,388	483	135	83	-	4,089
1799	5,936	905	198	117	11	7,167
1800	5,833	823	197	58	26	6,937
1801	5,500	667	123	67	42	6,399
1802	4,846	1,000	100	33	27	6,006
1803	4,816	1,692	133	67	23	6,731
1804	6,683	1,717	178	50	15	8,643
1805	-	-	-	-	-	-
1806	7,366	3,858	320	-	25	11,569
1807	2,000	2,000	133	-	3	4,136
1808	2,667	1,000	138	25	47	3,877
1809	433	753	37	-	-	1,223
1810	3,333	833	42	1,683	-	5,891
1811	8,333	3,367	343	3,167	16	15,226
1812	3,000	2,500	15	333	-	5,848
1813	2,333	2,500	100	58	43	5,034
1814	2,500	2,667	85	-	-	5,252
1815	3,528	3,000	220	8	10	6,766
1816	3,827	2,772	92	27	31	6,749
1817	6,075	2,233	155	750	47	9,260
1818	8,616	3,500	153	520	107	12,896
1819	867	2,143	77	-	120	3,207
1820	230	1,733	53	-	28	2,044
1821	1,035	3,358	140	-	7	4,540
1822	33	833	80	-	90	1,036
1823	405	2,010	125	-	105	2,645
1824	-	-	-	-	-	-
1825	-	-	-	-	-	-
1826	83	1,333	13	13	-	1,442
1827	333	3,333	200	-	18	3,884
1828	1,000	1,167	150	-	55	2,372
1829	150	667	23	-	28	868
1830	-	-	-	-	-	-
1831	750	1,042	50	-	8	1,850
1832	-	-	-	-	-	-
1833	-	-	-	-	-	-
1834	-	250	33	-	-	283

* "Other" includes peas, lentils, habas, and garbanzos.

Orchards

Mission San Juan Capistrano had a three-acre orchard just to the east of the Great Stone Church. It was surrounded by an adobe wall and had a building, probably for an orchard keeper and various implements. The wall was built in 1795 to protect against animals and poachers.

Unfortunately for history, the annual reports did not require a listing of orchard productivity, even when it was considerable. We do know, however, that the missions had a wide variety of trees providing olives, oranges, lemons, citrons, limes, peaches, pears, apricots, plums, apples, figs, and pomegranates. These trees produced their fruit at various times and provided a nice variety for the mission community.

Gardens

San Juan Capistrano also had a large vegetable garden, approximately six acres, just to the west of the mission's soldiers' barracks. It extended north beyond the west wing of the quadrangle and was completely enclosed with an adobe wall in 1793. It is believed young people, known as pajeros, helped the adults with the garden by shoeing away birds and other critters likely to damage it. They are said to have had a watchtower in the garden and would shout and make loud noises on a drum to scare away the pests.

Mission gardens were well taken care of and were prolific. They produced lettuce, cabbage, onions, tomatoes, chili peppers, asparagus, potatoes, artichokes, cauliflower, melons, pumpkins, garlic, and tuna (a cactus fruit of the prickly pear). These foods were not included in the reports, but caught the eye of early visitors to the mission who noted them in their writings.

Irrigation Works

Irrigation was key to the success of mission orchards and gardens. Over the years, a clever and extensive system was developed at Capistrano to direct water to wherever it was needed. It brought water for drinking, washing, and irrigation. Water was precious and every effort was made to make sure it was not wasted.

In 1779, Father Pablo Mugártegui reported from Capistrano that a zanja (ditch) had been dug to bring water to the garden from the Trabuco Creek on the west side of the Mission down to its garden. In 1809 this was refined with an aqueduct arch constructed just below the confluence of the Oso and Trabuco Creeks (located west of the modern J Serra High School). Remnants of the system were found in the excavations made for the old Capistrano High School just north of the Basilica Church.

As the Mission grew and expanded another water source was provided by creating a small reservoir, or pond, on the Horno Creek northeast of the Mission proper and southeast and across from the brick and tile kilns on Horno Street. This small creek used to run frequently, if not all the time. Traces of it may still be seen, but much of it has been changed by later grading and construction. Two zanjas were dug from it; one of them, the shortest, ran to the Mission where it split into several channels that ran across the mission grounds and emptied into the mission works and garden west of the quadrangle. It also had a branch that that ran to the orchard east of the Stone Church. Underground channels were made of fired ladrillos, or square tiles. Remnants of this system have been discovered during various excavations and construction work at the Mission and in other parts of the town. The other of the two zanjas leading south from the Horno Creek Reservoir went all the way to the large Mission Orchard and Vineyard southeast of the Mission. This system was created long ago, probably around 1785. It is amazing to see how well it worked long before the advent of modern, convenient, and readily available irrigation pipes.

The Mission, of course, like much of California, was subject to times of draught when water was scarce. Several wells were dug at the Mission over the years. One inside the quadrangle, another east of the Stone Church, and still another near the entrance to the Sala. These in their day became a convenient and reliable source of drinking water.

› *Horno Creek*

Vineyard

From the beginning, San Juan Capistrano had vine cuttings from Baja California ready for planting. Father Pablo Mugártegui wrote to Father Serra in 1779 that the vine cuttings had been buried to protect them from the winter cold. Afterwards, at the new mission site, they were planted in the garden just west of the Mission. It takes two years from the planting of the cuttings to produce fruit and about six years for the vine to mature. When Father Francisco Palóu in 1785 wrote his biography of Father Serra, his professor and mentor, he mentioned that San Juan Capistrano was already beginning to provide grapes for the table and wine for both Mass and the table.

A survey of San Juan Capistrano property in 1854 by John Cleal shows a vineyard just to the west of the Mission. Later, in the 1860 survey by Henry Hancock, this same area was described as the Mission garden and a thirty-acre area southeast of the Mission is described as the Mission Vineyard with an entrance avenue of olive trees. It seems that a small vineyard was included in the original garden west of the Mission until the larger property southeast was cultivated with vines and enclosed with an adobe wall.

We don't know exactly when, but we do know the Mission built a winery and also provided a building for storing its wine products. When pirates looted the Mission in 1818 some of them availed themselves to the wine and brandy to such an extent as to lose sight of their professional pirate duties. It is said that at this time two Indians drank themselves to death and another went insane. It is no surprise that under normal circumstances the missionaries kept the wine locked up and carefully monitored its use. What was not consumed at the table was stored and became a valuable trade commodity. Trade, of course, was not in the minds of pirates who excelled in simply taking.

In January of 1842, Duflot Mofras, a visitor to the Mission, wrote that he had heard that at one time the Mission had as many as five hundred barrels of wine and brandy, but, at the time of his visit, it had fallen to just fifty or sixty barrels. His numerical observations are considered exaggerated by historians in comparison with known facts, nevertheless he does provide a general idea of circumstances. That same year Father José Maria Zalvidea, who was at the Mission at that time, wrote to his superior, Father Narciso Duran, that the Mission Administrator, Don Augustin Olvera, "finds the Mission without wheat, wine, or brandy, with no wheat sown, and with the vineyard dried up." Be that as it may, there is no doubt that the Mission once possessed a large vineyard and winery. It prospered for a good number of years, but with the advent of secularization and government control, its products and the means of production went to ruin.

Olive Mill

Mission San Juan Capistrano, like the other California Missions, once had an olive orchard and an olive mill. Olives were produced for food and also crushed in an olive mill to produce olive oil. Both olives and their oil were used at the Mission. Their surplus also helped the mission community as valuable items for commercial trade.

Remnants of Mission Olive Mill c. 1890

Pirates

Argentina revolted against Spain in 1810, about the same time as the Mexican Revolution. It declared its independence in 1816, but bitter local rivalries led to a civil war between 1818 and 1820. Hippolyte de Bouchard, a Frenchman, who had served in the navy of the "Republic of Buenos Aires," took advantage of the upheaval in the Spanish Colonies to further his own interests. Under the color of patriotism, he in fact acted as a pirate and there was really no Spanish force to stop him.

Bouchard, in command of the ship Argentina, sailed to the Sandwich (Hawaiian) Islands, where he traded gold and silver objects looted from Latin American churches. While there he linked up with Peter Corney, an English soldier of fortune, who commanded the ship Santa Rosa. Together with a crew of three hundred and sixty cutthroats and ruffians, they decided to raid the Spanish controlled California Coast and seize whatever loot they might find.

California, however, got a warning about these plans when the American brig Clarion dropped anchor in Santa Barbara on October 6, 1818. News of the impending attack was sent immediately to Governor Pablo Solá in Monterey. He sent orders to all the coastal presidios and missions to prepare themselves and hide all their valuables at some safe place in the interior. California was on the alert – and worried too. They didn't have the men and arms to meet the threat.

On November 22, 1818 – one month and two weeks after the alert was raised – the Argentina and the Santa Rosa entered Monterey Bay. After a failed defensive effort, the Governor and his outnumbered men retreated inland. Bouchard's gang spent a week sacking the presidio and town. When there was nothing left worth stealing, they boarded their ships and sailed south along the coast. On December 2nd, they anchored off Gaviota, north of Santa Barbara, and plundered the Ortega family's Rancho de Refugio. They looted the place, burnt its buildings, and killed some of the cattle. Proceeding to Santa Barbara, they anchored for a time, but decided not to go ashore. They continued down the coast. Their next target was Mission San Juan Capistrano.

The missionaries, Father José Barona and Father Gerónimo Boscana, quickly gathered valuables, locked the Mission, and led the Mission Indians to refuge at their cattle ranch on the Plano Trabuco. The pirates, or so-called "Argentine Insurgents," looted the Mission on December 14th and 15th. It appears their principal mischief was to seize the Mission's stores of olive oil, wine, and brandy. What they could not take to the ship or drink, they smashed and poured out.

In later years, Peter Corney recalled this: "We again ran into a snub bay, in latitude 33 – 33 N, where we anchored under the flag of truce. The bay is well sheltered, with a most beautiful town and mission, about two leagues from the beach. The Commodore (Bouchard) sent his boat on shore, to say if they would give us an immediate supply of provisions we would spare their town; to which they replied, that we might land if we pleased, and they would give us an immediate supply of powder and shot. The Commodore was very much incensed at this answer, and assembled all the officers, to know what was best to be done, as the town was too far from the beach to derive any benefit from it. It was, therefore, agreed to land, and give it up to be pillaged and sacked.

"Next morning before daylight, the Commodore ordered me to land and bring them a sample of the powder and shot, which I accordingly did, with a party of 140 men, well armed with two field pieces. On our landing, a party of horsemen came down and fired a few shots at us, and ran towards the town. They made no stand and we soon occupied the place. After breakfast the people commenced plundering; we found the town well stocked with everything but money and destroyed much wine and spirits, and all the public property; set fire to the king's stores, barracks, and governor's house and about two o'clock we marched back, though not in the order we went, many of the men being intoxicated, and some were so much so, that we had to lash them on the fieldpieces and drag them to the beach, where about six o'clock, we arrived with the loss of about six men. Next morning we punished about twenty men for getting drunk."

His Majesty's California military prudently watched from a safe distance as they awaited reinforcements. By the time these arrived, the drunken patriots made their way as best they could to their ships and sailed down the coast. A confrontation was expected at San Diego, but the insurgents, probably considering the possible loot not worth the trouble, continued their voyage south and were not seen again in California waters.

Following the attack on Capistrano, there was an investigation during which the military and missionaries accused each other of failure to sufficiently protect the Mission. After a time, it was wisely determined that any real fault was attributable to the pirates. Peace prevailed and life at Mission San Juan Capistrano resumed its normal, blissfully unexciting pattern.

VIII Secularization

Spanish Policy

In 1492 the Indians discovered Columbus. European Colonization of the New World was off and running. Two hundred and seventy-seven years later, that movement reached Alta California with the Spanish Crown and Christian Cross freshly claiming San Diego, Monterey, and everything in between and far around. During those 277 years there had been plenty of time for Indian exploitation and abuse. Such behavior provoked outrage and called for Christian reform. Appeals were made to the royal conscience. The King claimed the Indians of the Americas as his subjects enjoying his majesty's protection. He and his council issued decrees respecting their rights and condemning those who would dare violate them. Of course, such virtuous decrees were issued far away from the front lines of culture clash, temptation, and opportunism. The implementation of these protective decrees, though well intended, was difficult and far from perfection. As in ages past and present, greed and cruelty found ways to ignore and circumvent justice.

Already in place before the cross and sword arrived in California, secularization was a Spanish policy designed to prosper the Native Americans and protect their rights. Secularization was not a bad word. It was intended to educate the Indians beyond survival and guide them to prosperity in the new civilization that was coming upon them. It sought to respect their land and to teach them how to use it best for their own welfare.

Moreover, it intended to uplift them from paganism to Christianity.

Secularization was not an arbitrary plan. It was Spanish policy. Through the missions, the Indians were to learn about the inspired teachings of Jesus Christ and be converted to Christian living. They were to be "civilized": learning Spanish, Spanish trades, agriculture, and ranching. They were to learn how to be peaceful, law-abiding, and loyal subjects of the King.

The Plan

Following the period of conversion and pacification, the missions were to be secularized. The converted and civilized Mission Indians would be assigned their private property and the means (cattle, etc.) to work them. Some of the land would be reserved for their town, or pueblo. The former mission churches would become parish churches with parish priests under the leadership of a diocesan bishop. Missionaries would leave and go out to new mission territories to carry on their ministry of evangelization. Spanish soldiers and settlers having endured the hardships of life on the frontier would be rewarded for their services with land grants. The King's extended kingdom was vast and there was plenty of land for all to thrive and prosper. Secularization looked good on paper and it had worked before. It was the system used successfully in the Mexican Sierra Gorda where Father Junipero Serra had served before coming to the Californias.

Presumptions

The reality of secularization in California did not live up to the ideal. There were various flaws. One of them was the presumption that Spain, or any other country, had the right to claim dominion over new territories by simply planting the flag and claiming it to be so. Of course, the Spanish like others considered the unexplored New World territories to be up for grabs, to be possessed on a first come basis. They considered the Indians as primitive, uncivilized, and ignorant of land ownership and use. It was thought that they would eventually understand and appreciate the benefits of absorption into the Spanish Realm. Besides, if Spain didn't take over the territory, some other country certainly would. A little "might-makes-right" concept entered into the rationale.

Another presumption was the missionization would be successful and not take too long. The question was left open as to when exactly a Mission Indian was truly Christian, civilized, and ready for an independent life. When would they be wise and strong enough not to be cheated and exploited by others? At the time this issue was forced politically and secularization was decreed, the Franciscans felt that the Indians were not ready for the change. The Indians had been generally successful in communal living at the mission, but on their own it seemed likely that they would be victims and perhaps revert to a primitive existence. On the other hand, the Franciscans could not say how long it would take to reach the point where secularization would succeed. Could the process be left so indefinite? The Californios were anxious for their rewards for service and wanted gifts of land. They envied the mission's material prosperity. It had been over sixty years since the missions began. How much longer must they wait?

Still another presumption was that there would be political stability during this process. This turned out to be far from the reality. In the beginning, it was not foreseen that the colonies in the Americas would break away from Spain and try to form their own independent nations. However, in later years colonials began to feel that Spanish rule was more a burden than a blessing. Their loyalty to Spain weakened as political stability also weakened within Spain. Most of the leaders in Mexico ("New Spain") were of Spanish blood, but most of the ordinary people were not. Many Spanish colonials had never seen Spain. Increasingly, the notion of independence gained popularity.

Revolution

The Mexican Revolution began in 1810 and disrupted Spanish control until 1822 when Mexican independence became a fact. Spanish policies, Spanish laws, and Spaniards themselves were all subject to the review and judgment of the Mexican government. California became Mexican territory. All this happened while the Spanish process of missionization to secularization was still in progress in Alta California. Ready or not, secularization was at hand.

Instability is hardly a strong enough word to describe the political situation in Spain in 1808. Chaos is probably more appropriate. King Carlos IV was forced by a liberal-minded Palace Revolution to renounce his throne in favor of his son, Ferdinand VII. Lured to France for "talks," Ferdinand was imprisoned by Napoleon. He was forced to abdicate in favor of his father who was in turn forced to turn over the throne to Napoleon's brother, Joseph Bonaparte. This triggered a civil war between Spanish nationalist liberals and Spain's new, conservative French leadership. The liberal nationalists organized its own government, an assembly known as the Cortes of Cádiz.

They elected from among themselves a regency of three to govern in the name of the imprisoned Ferdinand VII who was, for the most part, ignorant of their activities. The Cortes, predominantly influenced by the enlightenment ideas that inflamed the French Revolution, proclaimed a liberal Spanish Constitution on March 19, 1812. This was St. Joseph Day in the same year that Capistrano's Great Stone Church collapsed. Some might see a premonition of catastrophe in that coincidence. Be that as it may, on September 13th of the following year, the Cortes issued its Decree of Secularization for the Indian missions in Spanish America.

With Spain in disarray, her American colonies took advantage of the opportunity. In Mexico, Padre Miguel Hidalgo incited the Mexican Revolution on September 16, 1810. This struggle plunged Mexico into a decade long, bloody struggle of its own.

Meanwhile, Spanish and Allied Forces (principally British) drove the French from Spain in 1813. Napoleon was forced to release and restore Ferdinand VII to the throne of Spain. Once in power, he turned against his liberal supporters, cancelled the Constitution of 1812, and tried to restore an absolute monarchy. Angered liberal forces gradually accumulated sufficient power to stage a successful revolution in 1820. Although a humbled and pleading Ferdinand was allowed to retain his title as king, he was forced to accept the Constitution of 1812 and other liberal measures. This included the Decree of Secularization and the Reform Law of 1820 that harshly repressed the influence of the Church.

Because of Spain's struggle and the Mexican Revolution, it isn't surprising that communication between Spain and New Spain was highly disrupted. Fortunately for the California Missions, The Decree of Secularization and the Bando de la Reforma didn't arrive in Mexico until 1820. The Viceroy was surprised at these severe measures but was duty-bound to publish them on January 23, 1821. Nevertheless, he wasn't inclined to enforce these unpopular regulations. He already had greater problems to deal with. The Mexican Revolution had gained the upper hand. In fact, Spanish forces in Mexico were forced to capitulate in 1821. Mexico became free, independent, bankrupt, and unstable.

A Mexican Governor

In October of 1825, Governor José Maria de Echeandia arrived in California and set up headquarters in San Diego. He was California's first native Mexican governor and a strong advocate of secularization. One of his first actions was to send Lt. Romuald Pacheco to Capistrano and other missions to inform the Mission Indians that the new governor was their friend and recognized their freedom and equality. Naturally, the Indians liked the sound of that. From this time on, some of them became increasingly disorderly. In January of the following year, Corporal Hilario Machado reported a revolt at San Juan Capistrano. He asked for help to quell the trouble. Certain Indians had ordered him to put the Padre (Barona) in the stocks. If he didn't, they threatened to do it to him. Apparently, the threats were just threats, but the growing insubordination was obvious. In April of that same year (1826), the governor met with the missionaries of the southern district and informed them of his plans for emancipating the Mission Indians. They warned him to proceed cautiously. They had been in the missions for years and the governor had just arrived on the scene. They feared he did not foresee the problems that probably would result. The economy of the whole province depended on the productivity of the missins. The missionaries seemed to be the only ones who were able to manage the Mission Indians, to keep them together, and induce them to work. There was also the real possibility that the missionaries might depart. The Mexican government was not friendly to native Spaniards. Besides, some of the padres were ill and some were in their senior years. Some had already sought permission to retire. Who would replace them?

Emancipation

Governor Echeandia pushed ahead and on July 25, 1826, issued his Proclamation of Emancipation. In the missions from Monterey south, Mission Indians deemed capable of supporting themselves were free to leave the mission and, as Mexican citizens, free to do as they pleased within the law.

It wasn't long before complaints came back to Echeandia. Captain José M. Estudillo of the San Diego Presidio reported on April 25, 1827, that the Corporal of the Guard at Mission San Juan Capistrano complained to him of many robberies being committed by idle Indians who refused to work. The missionaries pleaded for help. They claimed that even when they begged the Indians to go to work, some of them would haughtily reply that they didn't have to because the governor said they were free.

On July 3, 1827, the well-meaning governor ordered San Juan Capistrano and other missions to establish primary schools for the Indians. This was a noble endeavor, but the mission, not the government, was expected to pay the salary of the teachers. It would do this, of course, but there was another problem: There were not enough people in the province who were qualified and willing to take on this employment.

On October 7, 1827, Governor Echeandia ordered an inventory of all the mission's possessions. This seemed unnecessary to the missionaries because at the end of each year they were already required to issue an annual report. The governor wanted more detail. This suspicious interest seemed to signal the intentions of certain Echeandia supporters who were covetous of the Indian mission property. The padres complied and sent in the information on December 22, but they were not unaware of what this was leading up to.

In spite of the fact that the emancipation program led to idleness, drunkenness, gambling, crime, and general disorder, the governor extended his proclamation to include the northern missions in 1828. He was bent on secularization and time was running out for him. He knew that the government in Mexico City was planning to replace him.

Governor José M. Echeandia

Watkins photo, 1876

Expelling Spaniards

It is often said, albeit cynically, that "No good deed goes by unpunished." As if the padres had not experienced enough humiliation at the hands of the secular authorities, the Mexican government, on March 20, 1829, issued a decree expelling all Spaniards in California, New Mexico, and the northern territories. They ordered the Spaniards to leave the country within a month and the republic within three months.

Even Governor Echeandia thought this unwise. He pleaded to allow the padres, such as Father Barona, to remain. He argued that these good men should be exempt because of their "age, infirmities, and virtue." Nevertheless, he published the decree on July 6, 1829. The decree was generally ignored; there were no replacements available; and without the missionaries the missions would collapse and the California economy along with them. Although the decree was insulting, the missionaries would have been happy to avail themselves of the opportunity to retire and spend the rest of their years in their native homeland.

Secularization Setback

The California proponents of secularization, eager to divide up mission property, received a setback when a more conservative Mexican government appointed Lt. Col. Mariano Victoria as the new Governor of California. However, Echeandia did not intend to leave office without accomplishing his goal of secularization. Even though Victoria had already arrived in California, Echeandia avoided him long enough to issue his Decree for the Secularization of all the missions on January 6, 1831. Victoria found out about this on his way up to Monterey. He immediately issued orders to prevent its publication, but that had already taken place in the north. On January 31st, Manuel Victoria took possession of his office in Monterey. The next day he annulled the secularization decree. He claimed it was illegal and not in accord with the policy of the Mexican government. Unfortunately, it is not recorded what he may have said to Echeandia.

Missionary opposition to secularization found short relief in Victoria's appointment. His strict military manner brooked no opposition. He soon made enemies of the restive Californios. They rose up in rebellion and sought to restore Echeandia to power. Rebels marched north. Victoria marched south. In a skirmish at Cahuenga, Victoria received a deep lance wound in the face. He decided California wasn't worth that much pain. On December 9th, he resigned his command to Echeandia. On January 17, 1832, Victoria left for Mexico on the American brig Pocahontas. He had governed in California less than a year, but for him – and his enemies – that was quite enough.

Echeandia was back in power, but he faced a rival in the north, Victoria's secretary, Captain Agustín Zamorano. He prepared for conflict by summoning to his side and arming Mission Indians from San Gabriel, San Juan Capistrano, San Luis Rey, and San Diego. Some even came from San Fernando. The fight never came. Having thought the better of it, he disarmed the Indians and sent them home. He settled with Zamorano, agreeing to rule in the south up to San Fernando while Zamorano controlled the north. This arrangement lasted until Mexico appointed a new governor.

San Juan Capistrano was back under the control of Echeandia, who drained it and San Luis Rey of much of its resources to support his ill-gotten rule. During this turbulent time frequent stabbings were reported at Capistrano as well as robberies and murders at San Diego. Mission order was breaking down.

Secularization Revived

In July of 1832, news arrived from Mexico that the government had appointed José Figueroa as the new Governor of California. But before Figueroa arrived, Echeandia issued

a formal proclamation to the four southern missions. In it he declared the necessity of secularization. He cited the Indians' enthusiasm for freedom. He claimed they were discontented with missionary rule and he hoped the padres would step down from administration and serve as religious curates. He also cited good results at San Juan Capistrano where the padre (Father Zalvidea) was ready to give up the burden of administration. Again, Echeandia was trying to force the cause of secularization before his successor arrived.

Father José María Zalvidea, alone at Capistrano, addressed a letter to Echeandia. The Franciscan historian, Father Zephyrin Engelhardt provides this translation:

"Although ill and burdened with so many sick, I make use of the spare moments left me to say that I desire nothing more than to be relieved of the temporal government of the Indians, because it has become very repugnant to us, and because I see the rationale of your Honor's plan, which should have been put into practice long ago, according to the orders and the plan of the Córtes of Spain. It is very advantageous to us missionaries personally. I served and managed the temporal and spiritual affairs of Mission San Gabriel for twenty-one years. Yet, after putting in all the stipends (annual allowance) as well as the money received as alms for the celebration of holy Masses, I left everything for the benefit of that community, and have not taken away as much as a half real. We are sons of obedience and, since we have been instructed by our Superiors that all orders and regulations of the civil and political government should come through the Superiors. I forwarded the Plan, which Your Honor had the kindness to communicate to me to the Father Presidente." (Echeandia had apparently ignored channels by dealing directly with the missionaries of the four southern missions in important matter regarding their ministry.)

Other padres were not as resigned to Echeandia's agenda as Father Zalvidea. Echeandia later wrote bitterly to his successor: "The conduct which the said missionaries of these four missions have manifested and are manifesting, the exception of Father Zalvidea, is the most vicious and reprehensible. Padre Sanchez, missionary of San Gabriel, died a few days ago, and in his place they have put Father Oliva, a subject of the King of Spain."

Mariano Vallejo, a Californio, later wrote in his memoirs that Echeandia did not have enough funds to travel back to Mexico. He states that Echeandia had to raise some $3,000 with the help of the missionaries at Capistrano and San Luis Rey. If Vallejo's memory is correct, it is ironic that he had to request help from these very men who had suffered so much under his regime.

General José Figeuroa arrived at Monterey on January 15, 1833, eight months after the Mexican government had appointed him Governor and Military Commander of California. In July, he visited Capistrano and the other southern missions. He wanted to see first hand their condition and judge what he could do to further the cause of the emancipation of the Mission Indians. Although he had hoped to divide up some of the mission lands among the Indians and give them their liberty, he was surprised to find that the Indians were not too enthusiastic about his ideas. They would still have to work the land and were not allowed to sell the property or allotted cattle and implements. Government overseers enforcing the plan would still curb their freedom. Many felt that if this is all that emancipation meant, they might as well still live the old way under the padres' management.

1876

1874

Decree of Secularization

Unconcerned about such seemingly minor problems, the Mexican government forged ahead with its plans for the territory. On August 17, 1833, it passed the Decree for Secularization of the Missions. There was no turning back. This was the law. Nevertheless, it would still be almost a year before it was implemented in California.

Meanwhile, Governor Figueroa was still trying to implement his plan of secularization at San Juan Capistrano where he believed conditions were the most favorable. He appointed Ensign José Rocha as commissioner for the task. Captain Pablo Portilla, Presidio Commander at San Diego, also became involved. He tried to apportion to the Indians the lands at Capistrano's San Mateo. In October, he wrote to the governor that the Indians resisted and wanted the lands nearest the mission which were already irrigated and under cultivation. Figueroa consented and by the end of the year it appears that nearly all of the Mission Indians had been emancipated and organized into an Indian Pueblo.

Emancipation was rapidly leading to secularization. In April of 1834, the Mexican government ordered Figueroa to implement its Decree of Secularization within four months. On May 1st, the governor presented the decree to the territorial assembly for discussion on how best to proceed. The Californios pressured Figueroa to allow others (presumably themselves), besides the Indians, to be included in any division of the mission lands. This was a major, but not unexpected policy change. Originally, secularization assured the Indians that the mission lands would be theirs alone. Now others, seeing the material success of the missions, wanted in on the action.

Emancipation, however, was continuing to reveal a host of problems. Capistrano was supposed to be a model of emancipation success. On the contrary, it was proving to be a disaster. The Indians interpreted their freedom as freedom from work. They ignored the authority of their mayordomo and even the urgings of their padre, Father Zalivdea. The fields, gardens, orchards, and livestock were being neglected in proportion to the dwindling number of workers.

Governor Figueroa, disturbed by the impending crisis, was inclined to blame Father Zalvidea. He so informed Zalvidea's superior, Father Narciso Duran, who on July 22, responded saying he had been down there to San Juan himself and seen the decline. He defended Zalvidea who he found to be "very exact in spiritual matters." He said, "I cannot bring myself to throw the blame on Father Zalvidea. All is owing to the insubordination of the Indians." He had witnessed it himself. Apparently, it was the policy and not the padre that created the problem.

California Decree

Even though these problems were evident at the other missions as well, the governor, though disappointed, seemed to regard the outcome as an inevitable resistance to change. Besides, he was under orders from the Supreme Government in Mexico and under pressure from the local politicos who demanded it. On August 9, 1834, he issued California's Decree of Secularization of the Missions. Under this law the former missionaries would serve in spiritual matters only. Secular authorities would take over the missions' material operations. A paid commissioner would oversee the implementation of the policy at each mission. A paid mayordomo, or foreman, would direct the Indians and enforce the commissioner's decisions. The property, both land and livestock, would be divided up. Each Indian family would have between 200 hundred and 400 varas square (183 and 367 yards square) of land. This land could be inherited, but not divided up or sold. If it was abandoned or not cultivated, it would revert to the Mexican nation. A sufficient portion of land would be designated as community property to pasture livestock. Community land would also be allotted for a pueblo, or town. Each family, according to its size, was to receive a share in the ex-mission's livestock, implements, and seed. The commissioner and the mayordomo were to see that the Indians continued to work for the community needs as well as for their own personal property. The mission buildings (except for the church, the padres' quarters, and the cemetery) belonged to the community for use as designated by the commissioner. Half of the livestock, implements, and seeds belonged to the community as a whole.

The commissioners possessed a lot of power over the ex-mission Indians and the former mission itself. It should not be too surprising that many of the members of the territorial assembly and their friends were appointed to this position. At San Juan Capistrano over the years, the commissioners included Ensign Juan José Rocha, José Antonio Pico (brother to Pio and Andres Pico), Francisco Sepulveda, Santiago Argüello, and Agustin Janssens.

Capistrano Inventory

The Secularization Decree prescribed that an exact inventory of ex-mission property be provided to the government. At Capistrano, Father Zalvidea and four special commissioners were appointed for this task: José Antonio Pico, José Antonio Fuentes, José Manuel Silva, and Ignacio Ezquer. They determined the value of all the mission property, including the buildings to amount to $54,456. The buildings alone were valued at $7,298. The Serra Church amounted to $1,250. The contents of the church and sacristy were estimated at $15,568. The padres' library – 209 volumes – came in at $490. Furniture, implements, and other items amounted to $14,707. And the outlying ranchos of San Mateo and Mision Vieja came to $12,019.

At the end of 1834, the first year of secularization, Ex-Mission San Juan Capistrano still had 861 Indians in its community. There were still 8,000 head of cattle, 4,000 sheep, 50 horses, and 9 mules. It also counted a relatively paltry 283 bushels of agricultural products, mostly corn. All these results for the year

36. Mission Bells, San Juan Capistrano.

were dramatically down from previous years, but they were soon to drop faster and more significantly.

In terms of spiritual results, measured only in the sacraments administered, there were just 17 baptisms and 9 marriages. The number of Christian burials for 1834 exceeded both and counted 39. This was yet another sign of a sadly and rapidly decaying community.

An Observation

Richard Henry Dana, author of *Two Years before the Mast*, arrived in California on January 14, 1835, and presented in his book an eloquent, contemporary description of events: "A law was passed stripping the missions of all their possessions, and confining the priests to their spiritual duties, at the same time declaring all the Indians free and independent rancheros. The change in the condition of the Indians was, as may be supposed, only nominal; they are virtually serfs, as much as they ever were; but in the missions, the change was complete. The priests have no power, except in their religious character, and the great possessions of the missions are given over to be preyed upon by the harpies of the civil power, who are sent there in the capacity of administradores, to settle up the concerns; and who usually end, in a few years, by making themselves fortunes, and leaving their stewardships worse than they found them. The dynasty of the priests was more acceptable to the people of the country, and, indeed, to every one concerned with the country, by trade or otherwise, than that of the administradores. The priests were connected permanently to one mission, and felt the necessity of keeping up its credit. Accordingly the debts of the missions were regularly paid, and the people were, in the main, well treated, and attached to those who had spent their whole lives among them; but the administradores are strangers sent from Mexico (incorrect), having no interest in the country; not identified in any way with their charge, and, for the most part, men of desperate fortunes, broken-down politicians and soldiers, whose only object is to retrieve their condition but a few years (months) before our arrival upon the coast, yet, in that short time, the trade was diminished, credit impaired, and the venerable missions were going rapidly to decay...Of the poor Indians very little care is taken. The priests, indeed, at the missions, are said to keep them very strictly, and some rules are usually made by the alcaldes to punish their misconduct; yet it all amounts to but little. Indeed, to show the entire want of any sense of morality or domestic duty among them, I have frequently known an Indian to bring his wife down to the beach, and carry her back again, dividing with her the money which she had got from the sailors. If any of the girls were discovered by the alcalde to be open evil doers, they were whipped, and kept at work sweeping the square of the presidio, and carrying mud and bricks for the buildings. Intemperance, too, is a common vice among the Indians."

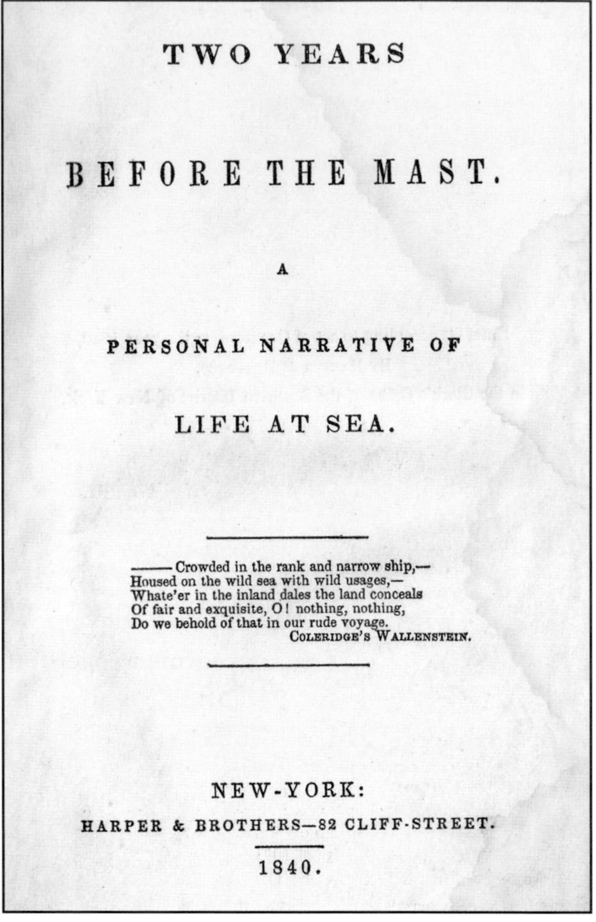

TWO YEARS

BEFORE THE MAST.

A

PERSONAL NARRATIVE OF

LIFE AT SEA.

——Crowded in the rank and narrow ship,—
Housed on the wild sea with wild usages,—
Whate'er in the inland dales the land conceals
Of fair and exquisite, O! nothing, nothing,
Do we behold of that in our rude voyage.
COLERIDGE'S WALLENSTEIN.

NEW-YORK:
HARPER & BROTHERS—82 CLIFF-STREET.
1840.

Death and Disruption

Governor Figueroa was himself in physical decline. He had not been very healthy since his arrival in the territory. In August of 1835, he took a medical leave of absence and placed the civil government in the hands of José Castro, the senior member of the assembly. He entrusted the military command to Lieutenant Colonel Nicolás Guttierez, the ranking officer. His health continued to worsen and, on September 29, 1835, he passed away at Monterey. In accord with his expressed wishes, his remains were interred with those of the Francicans at Mission Santa Barbara.

Following Figueroa's death, California fell deeper into political turmoil. José Castro served as governor pro tem for three months. Nicolá Guttierez continued as military commander and acted as governor until the regularly appointed governor arrived from Mexico, Mariano Chico. The Californios preferred one of their own. They treated Chico as an outsider. They forced him out of office and out of the territory in three months. Gutierrez resumed his role as governor and held on to the office for the next four months. All of this happened between October 1835, and October 1836. During this busy political competition, no one had time to keep a close eye on the activities of the mission administrators. That suited them just fine.

California Civil War

A quarrel over the customs service between Governor Gutierrez, who was a native Spaniard, and 27-year-old Juan B. Alvarado, a popular Californio, escalated into an armed rebellion. Alvarado ran Gutierrez out of the country. The territorial assembly without any authority from Mexico proclaimed Alvarado governor on November 7, 1836. The following year, on June 6th, Carlos Antonio Carrillo was appointed provisional governor. Alvarado liked his title and did not want to give it up. A territorial civil war ensued between Alvarado in the north and Carrillo in the south.

Both sides puffed up with patriotism and righteous indignation, called together their respective "armies." A confrontation occurred near San Juan Capistrano in what history calls the Battle of Las Flores, a rancho station just south of the ex-mission. Governor Carlos Antonio Carrillo with three cannons and about a hundred men took up defensive positions at the rancho. The northern army of about two hundred men, led by Juan Alvarado and José Castro steeled themselves for hand-to-hand combat with the enemy. They descended on ex-mission Capistrano, charging through its buildings with bayonets at the ready. The enemy wasn't there, just Ignacio Ezquer, temporary administrator, who was substituting for Francisco Sepulveda while he was serving with the southern forces. With Capistrano thoroughly conquered, Alvarado's troop occupied it and readied themselves for further glory. That opportunity presented itself on April 21, 1838. Alvarado's army drew up in battle array before Fort Flores and Carrillo's southern defenders. The roar of a defensive cannon boomed out once or twice from a position at the Flores corral. The nearly impotent shot had its deadly effect on some bushes and weeds. A flag of truce went up; negotiations ensued; and a treaty was signed. The battle of insults and war of words finally gave way to reason – diplomacy prevailed. Apparently, Carrillo blinked, because on April 23rd, Juan Bautista Alvarado was again the undisputed Governor of California. The Supreme Government of Mexico, exhausted by its own internal struggles and tired of territorial troubles, simply appointed Alvarado to the governorship he had usurped.

Governor Juan B. Alvarado 

A Padre's Plea

Back at Capistrano things hadn't gone too well. Poor Father Zalvidea, on August 27, 1837, pleaded with the governor for his passport. He wanted to return to Mexico City where he could "end his days quietly in his college." Alvarado refused. Capistrano needed its priest and Alvarado needed him there.

"Quiet" was the key word in Zalvidea's plea. On January 27, 1838, Santiago Argüello with his twenty-two children and relatives moved into the ex-mission. He was the new administrator succeeding Francisco Sepulveda. The inventory that accompanied the transition sadly indicated that the 8,000 head of cattle reported in 1834 had dropped in just four years to 494! The cattle had diminished but not the cost of running the ex-mission. Argüello's salary ($1,000) and the expense of supporting his family fell to the labor of Capistrano's emancipated Indians. They were not happy. It was difficult enough to support themselves. They resented supporting administrators, especially ones with big families. On April 8, 1839, they sent José Fermín Delfín as their representative to speak to the governor. Delfín charged Argüello with wasting and misappropriating the ex-mission property. He claimed that Argüello made the Indians cultivate "his" land; that he put his own brand on the best horses; and bought animals for himself with profit from the sale of brandy. The Indians were deserting. There were only 60 Indians remaining at work.

Mission Inspector

The complaints coming from Capistrano weren't the only ones. Reports of the conditions at other secularized missions were also dismal. Governor Alvarado appointed William Hartnell as Mission Inspector and sent him to investigate and report on what was going on. In mid-June of 1839, Hartnell arrived at Capistrano after inspecting San Luis Rey. On June 24, he reported to Alvarado that Capistrano had debts of $5,000. Pests had seriously damaged the vineyard and some 2,000 vine stocks had to be replaced. He found that there was a total of about 80 Indians left out of the 861 counted in 1834. Those remaining were very upset with Argüello. They wanted Vicente Moraga or Francisco Sepulveda to take over. Father Zalvidea confided to Hartnell that they would be even worse. The inspector determined that the Indian accusations against Argüello were exaggerated and unsubstantiated. He believed that some white troublemakers in the area had riled up the Indians and that these "whites" ought to be removed. Instead of being pacified, the Indians were further angered by Hartnell's refusal to accept their arguments.

Rented Indians

In August, a desparate Indian from Capistrano rode all the way to Alvarado's headquarters in Monterey – albeit on a stolen horse. He poured out this pathetic plea: "I am not an animal that they may make me work for masters who are not to my liking. You can do two things with me; either order me shot, if you wish, or give me liberty, if you are a just man. As for me, it is all the same. I am an old man and shall have to die soon anyway. You know that it matters little to me whether I die today or tomorrow."

A subsequent investigation revealed that mayordomos at the ex-missions had hired out their Indians to work on neighboring ranchos where they were cruelly treated and forced to work like slaves. As a result, the Monterey government issued a decree forbidding the practicing of renting Indians to outsiders.

1883

Administration Problems

Santiago Argüello defended his management by claiming he was unable to improve the state of affairs at Capistrano because of constant robberies and Indian desertions. Furthermore, the regional prefect would not allow the runaways to be arrested and brought back. (How can you operate a successful enterprise if your emancipated workers can't be forced to work?)

William Hartnell made a second visit to Capistrano in hopes of restoring order. Instead, he found the Indians outraged because Santiago Argüello was trying to put his son, Ramón, over them as mayordomo. There was no way that they were going to accept him. Santiago was not amused. Now it was his turn to be outraged. He protested, but to no avail.

The Pico Plan

The Pico brothers (Pio, Andres, and José Antonio) were interested in Capistrano. José Antonio had been an administrator there. They were already involved at San Luis Rey. Now Andres proposed that they rent Capistrano, pay its expenses, and hire the Indians who were willing to work. This plan was rejected. The Indians "owned" the ex-mission, why should they subject themselves to the renter? Father Narciso Duran wrote to Father Zalvidea on May 21, 1840: "One must be blind not to fear that the next step of the Picos will be to make themselves proprietors of the Mission with manifest hardship to the Indians."

Temporal Affairs

With the situation at Capistrano at a standstill, the California government decided to have Father Zalvidea take over temporary administration until arrangements could be made to turn the ex-mission into a pueblo. Father Zalvidea didn't really want to be associated with these "temporal affairs," doomed to inevitable failure. He in turn handed over the administration to Agustin Janssens, a respected man with more optimism than the beleaguered padre. Governor Alvarado approved this arrangement in January of 1841.

Pious Cattle

The missionaries, vowed to poverty, had always used their stipends (income) to purchase goods for the mission and the Indians. Even though the mission had been secularized, Father Zalvidea in his charity received permission to have his stipends applied to purchase cattle, 800 of them. This herd would serve as a kind of "Pious Fund," a charitable trust to finance the needs of the Indians, especially the poor and infirm. The herd's increase, like interest, would be the means of support. It was a good idea, but it ran into difficulties when others took over the needed pastures. These places had traditionally belonged to the Mission and were used for grazing its livestock. Now Santiago Argüello had his own cattle grazing on the Plano Trabuco. José Estudillo, who had also tried to lease Capistrano, had his cattle at the Mision Vieja pasture. Moreover, the Indians were beginning to complain to Father Zalvidea that they had heard rumors that "white" people were trying to get land grants in the area. The rumors were true.

The Pueblo San Juan De Argüello

In May of 1844, the governor determined to dissolve the Indian community at San Juan Capistrano and establish a pueblo open to both Indians and others. This was the first time that those who were not Indians – except for the missionaries, soldiers, and administrators and their families – would be allowed to populate Capistrano. The residents of San Diego were invited to petition for lands in the proposed pueblo. In June, Agustin Olvera was commissioned to distribute lands to the remnants of the Indians (about 100) and about 40 non-Indians. Rather pathetically, especially at this point, Agustín Janssens reported to authorities that worms had destroyed the crops and the Indians had gone away. He was out of a job.

In actuality, they hadn't all gone away. On July 11, Manuel Castañares reported to Alvarado that the only property belonging to the ex-mission consisted of five yoke of oxen. There were 26 married men, 7 widowers, and 5 unmarried men. It seems women and children were not considered relevant to the count.

On July 29, 1841, Governor Juan B. Alvarado issued regulations formally establishing the Pueblo of San Juan De Argüello. The new name testified to the influence of the Argüello family with the Governor. Juan Bandini became the commissioner in charge of making sure that all the regulations were observed. He wasn't pleased with the results. He resigned in disgust the following year.

A Bishop for California Bishop Francisco Garcia Diego y Moreno, O.F.M.

Although Father Francisco Garcia Diego y Moreno had been appointed Bishop of the Californias in April of 1840, it wasn't until October 4th that he was consecrated bishop in the Basilica of Our Lady of Guadalupe in Mexico City. Due to the need for extensive preparations, it was over a year before he took possession of his diocese. He arrived at San Diego, the seat of the diocese, on December 11, 1841.

The Franciscans had labored long and hard in the California Missions. They were now witnessing the disintegration of much of their work. Perhaps, it was thought, the bishop would have more political clout, could arrest the decay, and restore hope. In spite of the bishop's best intentions and efforts, he was frustrated at every turn. He didn't get the promised support from the Mexican government. Instead, it seized the Pious Fund, the financial basis for California's missionary work. Neither did he receive much more than suspicion from prominent, politically active Californios. Sadly, his presence didn't bring an end to the mission's decline. It just enabled him to personally witness more of it. After many disappointments and vexations, he passed away on April 30, 1846, less than five years after his arrival.

Ranchos
The Mission Divided

In 1837, the first major portion of San Juan Capistrano's mission lands went, not to the Indians, but to José Sepulveda whose father was the Mission Administrator. Governor Juan Alvarado granted the first installment to him on April 15th. A second installment, five years later, brought his Rancho San Joaquín (La Cienega) up to 48,803 acres.

On February 16, 1841, the governor provisionally granted the two square league Rancho Trabuco to Santiago Argüello, the former Mission Administrator, who in fact had already been using the land. On July 31st, the governor finalized the Trabuco grant, and in September, he declared the Ex-Mission Capistrano to be the Pueblo of San Juan de Argüello. Among the individual claimants in the new town were Santiago de Argüello, Ramon Argüello, and Santiago E. Argüello.

The mission lands were going fast. On May 3, 1842, Governor Alvarado granted Rancho Cañada de los Alisos to José Serrano, one of the claimants in the new pueblo. Across the valley, on May 13, he granted José Sepulveda the second installment to Rancho San Joaquín. Closer to town, on June 21st, the governor granted the 13,316 acre Rancho Niguel to Juan Avila, José Sepulveda's brother-in-law.

On July 30th, Father Zalvidea reported to his superior that there was virtually nothing left at the mission and that he was being supported by the kindness of Augustin Olvera, San Juan's Juez de Paz. By the close of the year, old and poor in health, he left for San Luis Rey. This left San Juan Capistrano without a resident priest for the first time in its seventy-three year history.

On July 5, 1843, Governor Manuel Micheltorena granted the area south of San Juan towards the ocean along San Juan Creek to Santiago Rios. Also during that year, John Forster purchased Rancho Trabuco from Santiago Argüello. The following year Forster moved into the mission. That same year, Pio

F. Fran.co Obispo De Californias.

F. FRANCISCUS GARCIA DIEGO * PRIMUS EPISCOPUS CALIFORNIEN. *

First Bishop's Seal.

and Andres Pico acquired Las Flores, once a thriving station of San Juan Capistrano. They added this to the 1842 grant of Santa Margarita y San Onofre, making them the largest land grant owners in California.

In 1845, John Forster purchased Rancho Mision Vieja (La Paz) from Augustin Olvera who had just received the grant on April 4th from Governor Pio Pico. On April 5th, Pico granted to Forster the Potreros de San Juan. And on December 4th, he purchased the Old Mission at government auction for $710 in goods. Two days later he received title to it from Pico who besides being governor, was Forster's Godfather and brother in law. That same year, Pico granted Forster the Rancho Nacional, a vast holding south of San Diego. Forster, who also acquired the nearly 10,000-acre Rancho San Felipe, soon became a major force on the California scene.

In the meantime, the Mexican Province of Alta California had been a political mess. Lack of control from Mexico and local rivalries had allowed factions to weaken the province and create a general atmosphere of uncertainty. In less than a year, there was war between Mexico and the United States.

In the closing months before the conflict, much of what was left of the former mission lands was parceled out. On April 21, 1846, Governor Pico extended Forster's holdings at Trabuco to three-square leagues. The next month, on May 7th, he granted the 6.6 thousand-acre Rancho Boca de la Playa, south of the mission, to Emigdio Vejar, a former mayordomo of San Juan. And on the 26th of May, to the north of the Mission, he granted the over 47,000 acre Rancho Lomas de Santiago to Teodocio Yorba. On July 7th, the U. S. flag was raised at Monterey and on September 7th, Pico escaped to Baja California. After the war, he quietly returned to reclaim his vast land grant holdings.

John Forster and his family resided at the Old Mission for twenty years. He later moved to the great hacienda on Rancho Santa Margarita (Camp Pendleton), which he acquired from Pio Pico in a bitter family lawsuit. He still claimed ownership of the Mission, but Bishop Sadoc Alemany challenged that before the U.S. Land Commission. The bishop won that case on the basis that the sale of the mission by Pico had been illegal under both Spanish and Mexican law. On March 18, 1865, President Abraham Lincoln granted a Patent of Title returning Mission San Juan Capistrano to the Church.

c.1880s

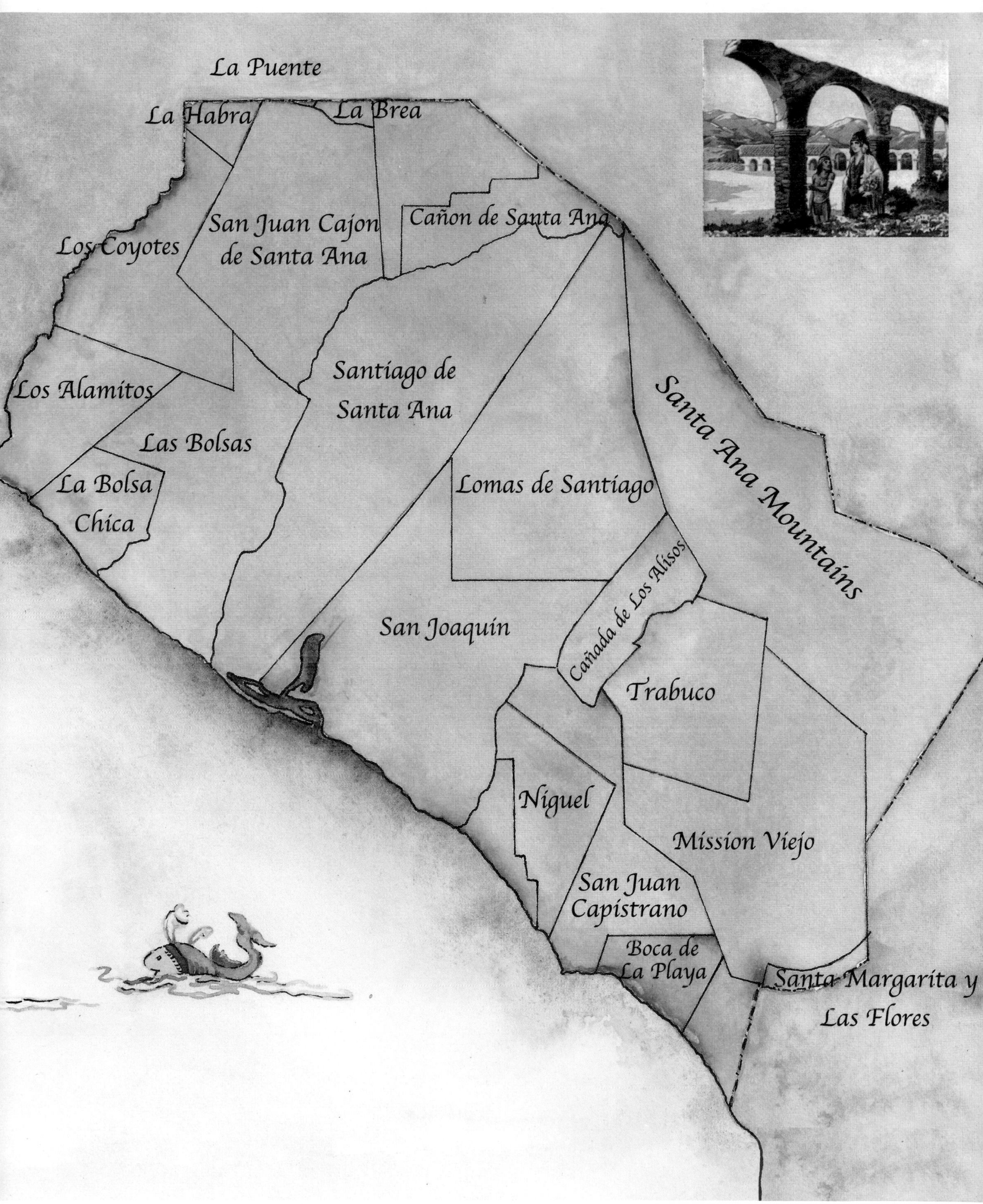
La Puente
La Habra
La Brea
San Juan Cajon de Santa Ana
Cañon de Santa Ana
Los Coyotes
Los Alamitos
Santiago de Santa Ana
Santa Ana Mountains
Las Bolsas
La Bolsa Chica
Lomas de Santiago
Cañada de Los Alisos
San Joaquin
Trabuco
Niguel
Mission Viejo
San Juan Capistrano
Boca de La Playa
Santa Margarita y Las Flores

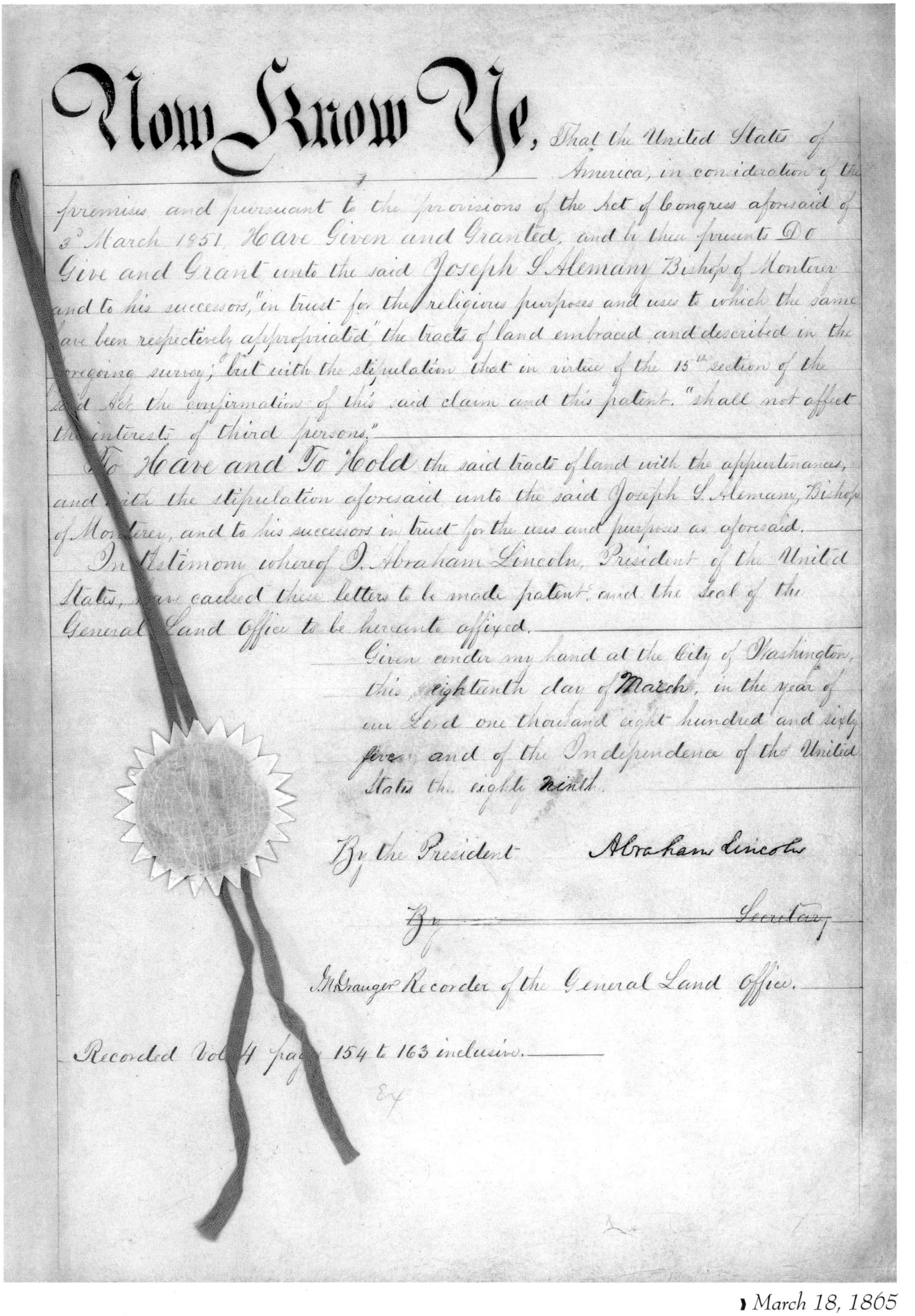

Now Know Ye, That the United States of America, in consideration of the premises and pursuant to the provisions of the Act of Congress aforesaid of 3^d March 1851, Have Given and Granted, and by these presents Do Give and Grant unto the said Joseph S. Alemany Bishop of Monterey and to his successors, "in trust for the religious purposes and uses to which the same have been respectively appropriated" the tracts of land embraced and described in the foregoing survey; but with the stipulation that in virtue of the 15th section of the said Act the confirmation of this said claim and this patent "shall not affect the interests of third persons."

To Have and To Hold the said tracts of land with the appurtenances, and with the stipulation aforesaid unto the said Joseph S. Alemany, Bishop of Monterey, and to his successors in trust for the uses and purposes as aforesaid.

In testimony whereof I, Abraham Lincoln, President of the United States, have caused these letters to be made patent, and the Seal of the General Land Office to be hereunto affixed.

Given under my hand at the City of Washington, this eighteenth day of March, in the year of our Lord one thousand eight hundred and sixty five, and of the Independence of the United States the eighty ninth.

By the President Abraham Lincoln

By ——— Secretary

J.N. Granger Recorder of the General Land Office.

Recorded Vol. 4 pages 154 to 163 inclusive.

March 18, 1865

Aftermath

Premature

The process of secularization presumed the converted Indians had become civilized and Christianized. The missionaries – their work accomplished – would move on to new frontiers and continue their mission of bringing Christ and His Word to new peoples. The former missions would simply become parish churches and secular clergy under a diocesan bishop would replace the missionaries.

Of course, secularization proved to be premature in California. The Mission Indians, for the most part, were not able to defend themselves against the aggressive schemes of the Californios who exploited them, seizing their lands and commanding their labor.

Secularization

Following secularization, the governors of California rapidly divided up and distributed the former mission lands in enormous land grants. These, of course, were not given to the Indians but to influential Californios. The governor generously rewarded his friends and, in the case of Pio Pico, was careful not to neglect himself.

The former Mission Indians generally scattered. Some went to find work in Los Angeles. Others took up employment at the new land grant ranchos. Some disappeared into the wilderness and took up life as in ancient times. A few stayed on near the Mission and worked their own small parcels of land meagerly granted them by the government. Still, some of the old and infirm remained about the Mission, unable to begin a new way of life. They relied for their subsistence on the government appointed administrator and the charity of the padre who, often enough, was at the mercy of the same salaried official.

Missionary Predicament

The Mexican government not only refused to allow new missionaries to come from Spain, they also sought to expel the existing Spanish missionaries. They didn't foresee the consequences. There were no secular priests to replace the Franciscan missionaries. The California economy, including the support of the military and the local government, depended upon the material success of the missions. Realizing this, the local authorities pleaded with the superior government to allow the Spanish missionaries to remain. By this time, however, the Spanish Franciscans were not all that eager to stay. Many of them were up in years and some of them were already in poor health. Besides, the obvious undoing of their years of hard work and the poor way in which they were being treated caused them to yearn for transfer and retirement to other more promising fields of ministry. Nevertheless, their sense of duty to the Indians and their vow of obedience kept them in place – many to die at their assignments.

Mexican Missionaries

Since the Spanish missionaries could not be replaced and missions were in danger of being without a priest, Church authorities in Mexico arranged for a number of native Mexican Franciscans to take up ministry in Alta California. With this reorganization, the Mexican Franciscans were assigned to the northern missions while the remaining Spanish Franciscans continued their labors in Southern California, including, of course, San Juan Capistrano.

A Diocese

In another attempt to remedy the situation, Mexican authorities changed the strictly missionary status of California. In 1840, Pope Gregory XVI, responding to a petition from the Mexican government, established the Diocese of Both Californias. For its care, he appointed Bishop Garcia Diego y Moreno, one of the Mexican Franciscan missionaries. The poor bishop soon discovered that the government's promised support turned out to be only promises. And, although he was able to enlist a few Mexican seminarians as prospective diocesan clergy, he was otherwise unable to find relief for the much-beleaguered California clergy.

Father Zalvidea

Father José Maria Zalvidea had the bitter experience of enduring the unrelenting decline of the Mission from its prosperity to its disintegration. He had arrived at Capistrano in 1826 and served with Father José Barona who had been there since 1811 and seen the height of the Mission's success. But when Barona died in 1831, Father Zalvidea was left at the Mission by himself and there was no one else who could be sent to assist him. That was the first time since the Mission's founding in 1776 that only one priest was assigned to San Juan Capistrano.

Father Zalvidea pastored the Mission eleven more years under deplorable conditions. In 1842, he transferred to San Luis Rey where its only priest, Father Francisco de Ibarra, had passed away. Father Zalvidea was not replaced at Capistrano. The Mission was left to the occasional care of San Gabriel.

U.S. – Mexican War

Mexican California was not destined to remain Mexican for long. Mexico, since its independence from Spain, had fallen into chronic political chaos. Little attention and less support was paid to its distant California Province which became increasingly beset with its own political turmoil. A weakened Mexico and its still weaker territories became ripe for conquest.

The United States, convinced of its Manifest Destiny, had set its sites on the American Southwest and the Pacific Coast. In the 1830s, it had offered to purchase Texas from Mexico. Although this proposal was declined, Anglo-Texan settlers moved toward independence and, in fact, declared it in 1836. The ensuing conflict brought defeat to the Mexican military and established the Republic of Texas. In spite of its defeat, Mexico didn't recognize Texas independence. The United States continued it efforts to purchase Texas, but its offers were rebuffed. A crisis emerged when Texas was annexed by the United States and Congress accepted it as a new state in the Union. Hostilities soon followed. On April 25, 1846, the Mexican army attacked a U.S. patrol, killing some of its men. On May 13, the U.S. Congress declared war on Mexico. President Polk, anticipating – if not orchestrating – the war, had already directed the U.S. Pacific Naval Squadron to seize California's ports as soon as they received word of the war. Commodore John Drake Sloat captured Monterey on July 7, 1846.

The Californios were not unaware of the impending conflict. Prior to the war, land grants were hastily handed out in an effort to establish future legal claims. It was during this time that Governor Pio Pico sold some of the California missions. San Juan Capistrano was one of them.

His brother-in-law and Godson, Juan Forster, acquired it in December of 1845.

San Pasqual

The only significant – and bloody – battle of the U.S. – Mexican War in California took place near the Indian village of San Pasqual (San Diego County) on December 5, 1846. It was a temporary victory for the Californios. Following the battle, some of the wounded Californios were brought to the Forsters at Capistrano where they were hidden and given medical treatment.

1897

Father Oliva: Last of the Missionaries

In the fall of 1846, Father Vicente Oliva took up residence in the padre's quarters next to the Forster family at San Juan Capistrano. It had been nearly three years since a priest had lived there. Sadly, Father Vicente was already old and infirm. He lived there only a year and four months, passing away on January 2, 1848. He was buried in the sanctuary of the Serra Church.

Two things stand out as especially noteworthy about Father Vicente Oliva's brief ministry at San Juan Capistrano. First of all, he served there during the uncertain and dangerous times of the U.S. – Mexican War. And secondly – and sadly, he was the last of the Franciscan missionaries to reside at the Old Mission. Spiritual care of Capistrano once again fell to San Gabriel which occasionally sent priests down to tend to the communities needs.

Last Mexican Governor

Following the U.S. invasion, Governor Pio Pico hid out near San Juan Capistrano. No doubt Juan Forster, his brother-in-law, assisted him. Afterwards, Pico slipped across the border into Baja where he remained until hostilities cleared. The war came to an end in 1848 with the Treaty of Guadalupe-Hidalgo. This treaty guaranteed that the land grants given under Spanish and Mexican law would be respected, but the grantees had to prove their title with the appropriate documents. Former Governor Pico, when he thought it was safe, slipped back into California to claim his own extensive land grant. He is said to have helped some of his friends by post-dating land grants for them.

U.S.A.

Major changes occurred rapidly in California. In 1848, it became a U.S. possession. That same year gold was discovered and the following gold rush brought in thousands of foreigners, many who took up permanent residence. (California was no longer just a Spanish-speaking territory.) Furthermore, in 1850, on September 9th, California achieved statehood. Ex-Mission San Juan Capistrano humbly carried on in the midst of all these momentous events.

Father Rosales

In 1850, the year of California Statehood, Father José Maria Rosales took up residence at San Juan Capistrano and became its first diocesan priest. He had come up from Mexico as a seminarian with the newly appointed Bishop Garcia Diego. He was ordained a priest at Santa Barbara in 1843 and served at San Buenaventura until 1848. Following that assignment, while he was returning to Mexico, he took pity on the people of Capistrano who had been without a priest for two years. With diocesan permission, he moved into the old priests' quarters next to the Forsters and became pastor of San Juan Capistrano. He was enthusiastic about the Capistrano community, proud of his stature as its first diocesan priest, and well received by the people. After serving there for three and a half years, it seems his longing for his homeland prevailed. When he first came to California, it was Mexican, but with the change to American rule he wanted to go home. With the bishop's permission, he left in 1853.

Father José Maria Rosales

A Small Community

It should be kept in mind that San Juan Capistrano was a very small community at this time. When it was an Indian Mission, it once boasted of over a thousand inhabitants, as a parish in the 1850s it consisted of Californio Ranchero families and a few remaining Indians. In his account book, Father Rosales counted twenty-three persons who lived in the town or at nearby ranchos. Presumably, most of these were heads of families. Those listed may be considered as some of Capistrano's earliest pioneers. They are: Teodósio Yorba, Ramón Carrillo, Leandro Serrano, Pedro Antonio Ramón Yorba, Domingo Soledad Yorba, Catalina Yorba, José Sepulveda, Juan Avila, José Serrano de los Alisos, Emígdio Vejar, Santiago Rios, José Alipás, Manuel Manríquez, Pedro Verdugo, Meregildo Olivárez, Miguel Yorba, Francisco Rodríguez, Juan Forster, Pio Pico of San Mateo, Blas Aguilár, Silvério Rios, Antonio Maria Olivárez, and Manuel Niéves Felix.

Bishop's Petition

In 1851, the United States Congress set up a Land Commission to verify land claims in the State of California. In 1853, Bishop Sadoc Alemany, O.P., then the Bishop of Monterey, entered a petition before the Land Commission seeking the restoration of the California Missions to the Church. In the case of San Juan Capistrano, the argument was made that Governor Pio Pico had illegally sold the Mission contrary to the existing laws of both Spain and Mexico. It would take twelve years for the U.S. government to review and settle the issue.

Father Bagaria

Father Pedro Bagaria replaced Father Rosales at San Juan Capistrano. He was a Spaniard ordained by Bishop Alemany in 1853 and Capistrano was his first assignment. Like Rosales before him, he resided in the padre's apartment next to the Forster's residence. He served the Old Mission for three years, after which the bishop granted his request to leave the diocese.

Father Vila

Following Father Bagaria's departure, Bishop Thaddeus Amat, C.M., then Bishop of Monterey, assigned Father Jayme Vila to San Juan Capistrano. He was a Spaniard, ordained priest in California by San Francisco Archbishop Alemany in 1855. After serving briefly at San Gabriel, he served even more briefly at San Juan Capistrano – just three months! He arrived in October of 1856 and departed at the end of December when Bishop Amat made him a pastor in San Diego.

Father Molinier

In 1857, Bishop Amat replaced Father Vila with Father Jean Molinier, a native of France. He had come to California in 1852 and initially served the spiritual needs of gold rush immigrants at Mariposa. Later, he served as pastor of Mission San Juan Bautista and San Salvador in Jurupa, San Bernardino County. After ministering at San Juan Capistrano for two years and two months, he transferred to San Diego in the spring of 1859.

It is noteworthy that Father Molinier was newly arrived at Capistrano when the bandit Juan Flores and his gang shot up the town, robbing the Krasewski store and killing George Pflugardt, a merchant. Later, the same gang ambushed and killed Sheriff Barton. A posse pursued Flores and brought him to justice. He was subsequently hanged in Los Angeles.

Growth

The population of San Juan Capistrano, though still small, was slowly growing beyond its Indian and ranchero inhabitants. This was true of most of the State. Some came from Mexico – "Sonorans," as they were called. Others, either on their way to or returning from the lure of the gold fields, settled down to a less adventurous but more dependable life in rural, agrarian Southern California. In 1858, the town of Anaheim was laid out for a colony of Germans venturing into the grape and wine business. That same year Don Bernardo Yorba passed away and deeded to Bishop Amat land for the San Antonio Church and cemetery. Slowly, but steadily, new faces and new nationalities were adding to the Southern California community.

c. 1890s

Father Llover

Father Vicente Llover replaced Father Molinier at Capistrano in April of 1859. He was a Spaniard who came to California in 1854 and was ordained a priest by Bishop Amat on March 19 (St. Joseph Day) in 1856. His first assignment was at Our Lady Queen of the Angels Church (the Plaza Church) in Los Angeles. Later, he was sent to Mission San Buenaventura. When he arrived at San Juan Capistrano in 1859, it was his third assignment in the three years since his ordination. His assignment at Capistrano included (as needed and in case of emergency) San Luis Rey, San Diego, and the Indian community at Pala.

As a neighboring clergyman, Father Llover was present on April 29, 1860, when the Very Reverend Blas Raho, C.M., Vicar General, blessed the San Antono Church at the Yorba Rancho on the Upper Santa Ana.

Toward the end of 1862 and the beginning of 1863, Father Llover ministered to the Indians during a small pox epidemic during which 130 Indians died. He wrote in the burial register, " As I was occupied assisting the dying, I could not fix the date in the case of everyone."

The experience must have been overwhelming. Shortly after the epidemic, he himself became ill. On February 6, 1863, Bishop Amat granted his request to return to Spain.

Father Duran

Father Miguel Duran was thirty-two years old when he replaced Father Llover in August of 1863. As a Spanish seminarian he volunteered for California. Bishop Amat accepted him and had him finish his studies in Spain. Cardinal Barnabo of the Congregation for the Propagation of the Faith ordained him to the priesthood in 1859. Father Duran arrived in Los Angeles in 1860 and was assigned to Our Lady Queen of the Angels in Los Angeles. In 1863, Bishop Amat gave him the unusual assignment of ministering for several months to former Mission Indians and other Catholics living along the west side of the Colorado River. On his return, the bishop sent him to Capistrano. Like Father Llover before him, he also had charge of San Luis Rey, Pala, and San Diego. It was during his time at the Mission that the Forster family moved out and took up residence in the hacienda at Rancho Santa Margarita (Camp Pendleton). Although he may not have been aware of it, it was also during his ministry at the Old Mission that President Abraham Lincoln signed the Patent of Title restoring San Juan Capistrano to the Catholic Church on March 18, 1865.

Father Duran served at Capistrano for three years. At his own request, he asked to return to the Queen of Angels Church in Los Angeles. He was granted this permission in August of 1866.

Father Mut

Since 1842, seven priests served successively at San Juan Capistrano. None of these stayed as long as four years. One of them stayed only three months. Certainly, it was not a prize assignment – if there were any in the diocese at the time. The prospect of serving alone in a disintegrating ex-mission and being responsible for the spiritual welfare of Catholics spread out over a very wide area was more than a little daunting. The expectation of financial support was next to nothing. Anyone who came to minister at San Juan Capistrano had to be motivated purely by the desire to serve as a humble minister of Christ.

In 1866, Bishop Amat sent such a person to Capistrano – Father Joseph Mut. He was one of those the bishop had personally recruited for California from Spain. He made his way to the United States while the American Civil War was going on. He arrived at the Vincentian College at Cape Girardeaux, Missouri, where he completed his studies, presumably also learning some English. Afterwards, he continued on to California where Bishop Amat ordained him to the priesthood on December 12, 1862. His first assignment was as assistant pastor at Queen of Angels Church in Los Angeles. This was the bishop's cathedral and a place where the newly ordained could experience the priestly ministry under the bishop's close observation. Father Mut's service at the Plaza Church was highlighted by his zealous pastoral care of the sick during a small pox epidemic.

After this four-year internship, Bishop Amat sent Father Mut down to San Juan Capistrano as its pastor. He also was charged with the care of San Luis Rey, Pala, and other Indian settlements down to San Diego.

During his time, many of the land claims were being investigated and settled. He is said to have been a strong advocate of the Indians, who often were the victims of greedy individuals who ignored or challenged their rights. Of course, this advocacy earned him some enemies who later sought to have him removed.

Although Lincoln's Patent of Title had already been granted, records show that as late as 1875 the Church's claim to ownership of the Mission was still being challenged in court. The filing of the Patent at the Los Angeles County Records Office finally put an end to the litigation.

Because of Father Mut's jurisdiction over San Luis Rey, it ironically fell to him to bless the grave of José Antonio Pico, the brother of former Governor Pio Pico who had attempted to sell Mission Capistrano.

Although there are no remaining records of any special centennial celebration, Father Mut was at the Mission when it completed its first hundred years on November 1, 1876. Perhaps its condition didn't seem to warrant much celebration at the time. Photos taken in 1876 show the Old Mission in a lonely and desolate state.

With much of the place falling down around him, Father Mut must have been constantly involved in clean up and repairs. Sometime during his pastorate the roof above the sanctuary of the Serra Church collapsed. Since the congregation was small anyway, he simply put up a new adobe wall to meet that part of the roof that was still intact. It was a practical decision, but it left the old sanctuary and the graves of the priests outside of the building where – open to the elements – it gradually dissolved into muddy ruins.

Father Mut lived in the old padres' quarters in the south wing of the Mission. The place was noted for its utter simplicity. For safety, he had a second story built over the original apartments. Father Zephyrin Engelhardt, O.F.M., who visited the place in 1904, remarked that access to that upper level consisted simply of a rickety ladder. In some respects, he lived in greater poverty and more humble circumstances than some of the original missionaries.

Father Mut served at San Juan Capistrano for twenty years. This continuous ministry brought to the community a much-needed spiritual stability. It hadn't had that for many years.

In 1886, Bishop Francisco Mora, then Bishop of Monterey-Los Angeles, transferred Father Mut to Mission San Miguel. He had served Capistrano for a long time and had witnessed many changes. Although not always appreciated, his humble and faithful ministry provided a steady presence as the old ways progressed, sometimes painfully, to a new time and a new generation. Father Joseph Mut passed away at San Miguel in 1889 and is buried in its cemetery next to the mission church.

Father Duran Again

In a rather unusual turn of events, Father Miguel Duran replaced Father Mut at the Old Mission. It may be remembered that he had served at Capistrano twenty years previously. This time, however, he was in very poor health. He had old friends in town who helped take care of him. He carried on as best he could, but passed away in 1889, the same year as Father Mut.

Father Joseph Mut

No Resident Priest

One of the things significant about Father Duran's passing is that the bishop decided not to replace him. For the next twenty years Capistrano would be without a resident priest. It became a mission station occasionally visited by priests from Anaheim and Santa Ana.

In 1893, Franciscans once again staffed Mission San Luis Rey. Father Joseph Jeremiah O'Keefe, their administrator, tended to San Juan Capistrano for the next nine years. He used to come up twice a month to celebrate Mass and take care of baptisms and other spiritual needs.

During Father O'Keefe's time, the Serra Church became dangerously unstable. As a result, the Sala (today's gift shop) was remodeled into a church in 1891. This remained Capistrano's church until 1924.

With Father O'Keefe's departure to Santa Barbara in 1903, Capistrano again fell to the care of Anaheim and Santa Ana. In 1905, the bishop considered arranging with the Franciscan Province to take over San Juan Capistrano. For five years Franciscans came down by train from Los Angeles to provide Mass at the Mission. However, in 1910 an unexpected opportunity occurred which changed the plan.

Father Joseph Jeremiah O'Keefe, O.F.M.

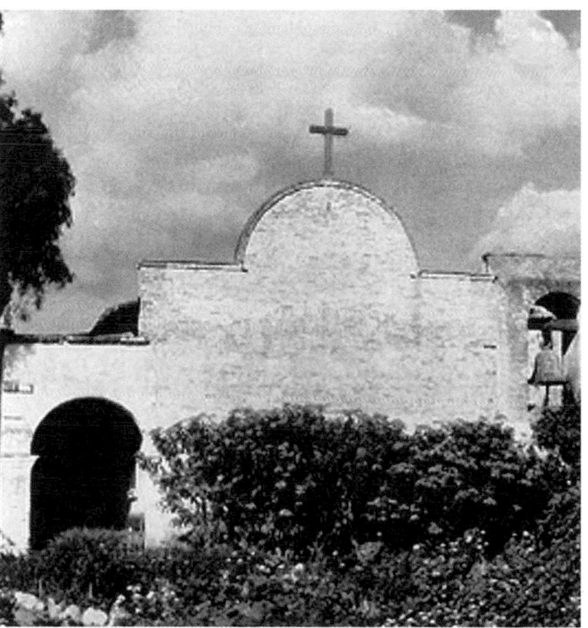

Sala remodled into a church in 1891

The Sala remodled into the church

Father Quetu

In 1910, Father Alfred Quetu arrived in Capistrano with relatives who had purchased a local ranch and hoped to succeed in the agricultural business. The locals referred to them as the French Colony. Father Quetu was French and had retired from his semi-missionary labors in Arizona. Since he lived near the Mission, he suggested to the bishop that he might provide Mass at the Mission every Sunday. He said that his age and health did not permit him to do much more, but at least this would be an improvement over the current twice-a-month schedule. The bishop accepted and appointed Father Quetu as the Mission's rector.

Perhaps the single most important contribution made by Father Alfred Quetu for the Mission was his success in talking young Father St. John O'Sullivan into coming to Capistrano and helping out at the Mission.

Father O'Sullivan

Father St. John O'Sullivan was born in Limerick, Ireland, on March 19 (St. Joseph Day), 1874. His family moved to the U.S. and settled in Louisville, Kentucky. Following studies at Notre Dame and at the seminary in Rochester, New York, he was ordained a priest for the Diocese of Louisville on June 12, 1904. Unfortunately, before long he contracted tuberculosis. His doctors recommended that he find a better climate in the hope of improving his health. With his bishop's permission, he headed west. He spent some time in Texas and then moved on to Arizona where, gravely ill, he wound up in a hospital run by Father Quetu's sister who was a nun. It was there that he first met Father Quetu. After sufficiently regaining his health, Father O'Sullivan traveled to California and was at San Diego when Quetu invited him up to help out at the Old Mission.

Although he was very ill when he arrived at Capistrano by train in 1910 (It is said he had to be carried to the Mission from the depot.), he gradually got better and his disease went into remission. As he regained his health, he fell in love with the historic Mission and its people. He quickly learned Spanish and took a lively interest in gathering up the Mission's stories from the townspeople. His enthusiasm for restoring the Mission was infectious. Before long, he had a steady group of volunteers working with him to repair and restore the venerable Old Mission to its proper dignity.

In 1914, Father O'Sullivan succeeded Father Quetu as pastor. Quetu was already semi-retired anyway. World War I had dearly cost his family's holdings in France. The ranching venture in Capistrano met with a series of reversals. Belford Terrace, the main house, burned down in an electrical storm in 1910. By 1914, Father Quetu was ready to move on and was confident that his friend, Father O'Sullivan, could manage things quite well. The bishop agreed with this assessment and appointed Father O'Sullivan as full time pastor. They were not to be disappointed. The young priest served the Mission successfully for twenty-three years. He won the respect and admiration of most who had the privilege of knowing him. Sadly, his health problems chronically reoccurred. Each time he managed to recover, but in 1933 he no longer had the strength to carry on. In June of that year, Bishop John J. Cantwell arranged with Pope Pius XI to bestow on him the honor of Domestic Prelate with the title of Monsignor. Shortly afterwards, on July 22nd, Monsignor St. John O'Sullivan passed away at St. Joseph's Hospital in Orange.

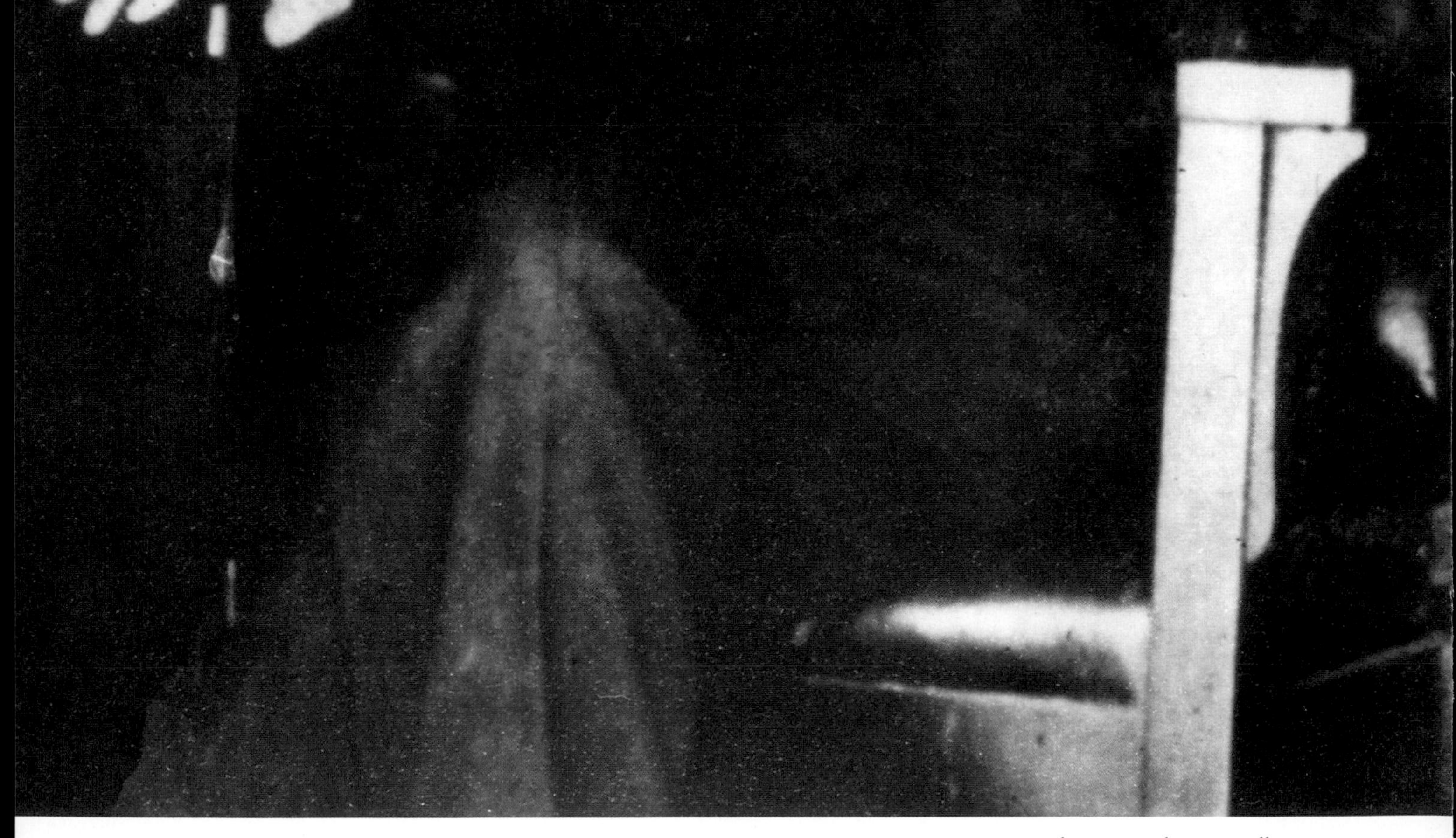

Father St. John O'Sullivan

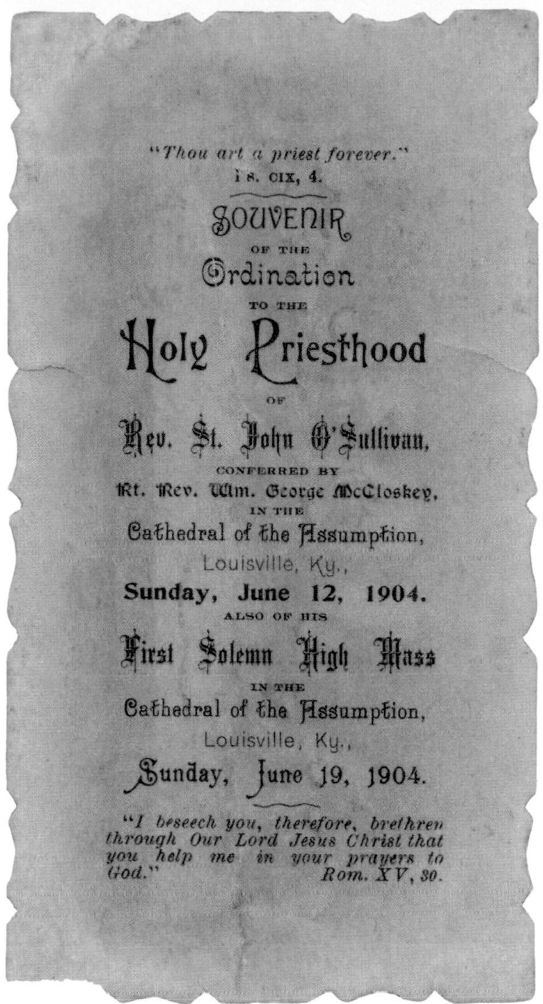

"Thou art a priest forever."
Ps. cix, 4.

SOUVENIR
OF THE
Ordination
TO THE
Holy Priesthood
OF
Rev. St. John O'Sullivan,
CONFERRED BY
Rt. Rev. Wm. George McCloskey,
IN THE
Cathedral of the Assumption,
Louisville, Ky.,
Sunday, June 12, 1904.
ALSO OF HIS
First Solemn High Mass
IN THE
Cathedral of the Assumption,
Louisville, Ky.,
Sunday, June 19, 1904.

"I beseech you, therefore, brethren through Our Lord Jesus Christ that you help me in your prayers to God." *Rom. XV, 30.*

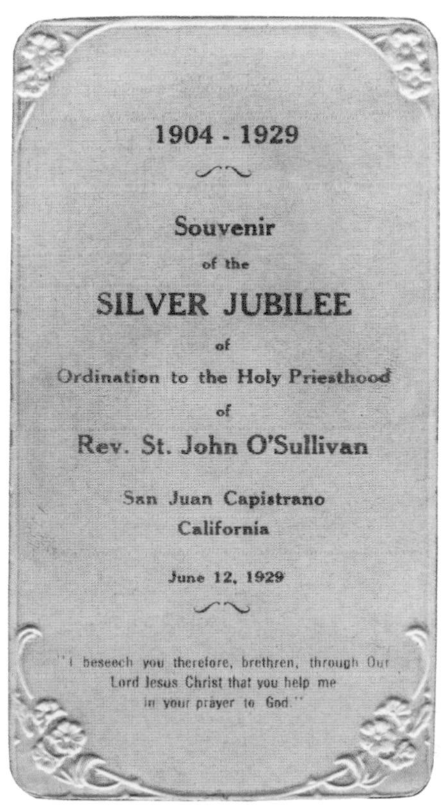

1904 - 1929

Souvenir
of the
SILVER JUBILEE
of
Ordination to the Holy Priesthood
of
Rev. St. John O'Sullivan

San Juan Capistrano
California

June 12, 1929

"I beseech you therefore, brethren, through Our Lord Jesus Christ that you help me in your prayer to God."

Pioneer restorer of the Mission

Rev. Monsignor St. John O'Sullivan (1874 - 1933)

Preservation & Restoration

In the Beginning

From the very beginning of Mission San Juan Capistrano there was building and rebuilding. Flimsy, temporary structures gave way to stronger, better, more suitable buildings. The initial buildings at the first mission site were abandoned in 1778 when the mission was relocated to its present site where there was a more dependable water supply. The original structures of 1776 were so inadequate that they quickly went to ruin and have long since disappeared.

At the new site every year marked building progress. Even so, all during the mission period there was still the constant need of maintenance and repair. As buildings became older, they were taken down and replaced with new facilities more suitable for the growing mission population.

Bricks and Tiles

One of the greatest changes in mission building came with the need to provide better roofing for its structures. For years roofs of timber, earth, and tule left the structures vulnerable to the hazards of weather, rot, and fire. The advent of brick and tile kilns (c. 1788) proved to be a major practical and ascetic improvement. Nevertheless, even these new roofs would have to be replaced from time to time.

1812

Some problems proved beyond repair. Since the 1812 earthquake, San Juan Capistrano's most impressive building, the Great Stone Church, has stood in its ruined state as a testament of human endeavor humbled before forces beyond its vision or ability to control.

Secularization

There was never a time in the Old Mission's history when preservation and restoration were not factors in its continuing existence. However, the greatest challenge came with secularization. Prosperity gave way to decline when the lands were divided and the Indians were scattered. Diminished resources led to inevitable neglect while time, nature, and occasional vandalism threatened to eradicate the once thriving complex.

The long period of decline, some six decades, almost equaled the mission period's time of growth and prosperity.

Rehabilitation

Finally, by the 1890s people began to recognize the cultural and historic value of the old California Missions. They saw that if something wasn't done soon, these treasures would be lost. Visionaries like Charles F. Lummis, the founder of the Landmarks Club, and Father St. John O'Sullivan, Pastor of the Mission, did everything within their powers to restore Mission Capistrano to its dignity. By their personal efforts and enthusiasm they were able to gather around them the human and other resources required to make their dream of preserving and restoring the Old Mission a reality. Others have followed who have continued this work and have made the Mission the beautiful, historic, and educational landmark it is today.

Preservation and Restoration

1887 The railroad extends through Capistrano from Los Angeles on its way to San Diego.

1889 Orange County separates from Los Angeles County.

1891 The Sala (reception room) at the front of the Mission is remodeled and becomes the church for San Juan Capistrano. The old Serra Church had become dilapidated and too dangerous for services.

1895 Under the leadership of Charles Fletcher Lummis, the Landmarks Club incorporates as a non-denominational, non-profit organization dedicated to the preservation of the California Missions and other decaying historical treasures in danger of destruction. Mission San Juan Capistrano is its first project.

1896 In order to strengthen its non-denominational status in soliciting donations, the Landmarks Club secures a ten-year lease of Mission San Juan Capistrano from the Diocese of Monterey-Los Angeles.

1896 The Landmarks Club begins critical preservation work at Mission San Juan Capistrano:

The mission kitchen is repaired Its vaulted roof is strengthened with iron tie-rods. Breaches in its walls are repaired. New door and window frames are installed.

The south wing (the front building) is re-roofed. The western end wall is rebuilt.

The corridors of the south wing, front and back, are re-roofed.

Leaning colonnade pillars are straightened.

At the Great Stone Church a new foundation is provided for a threatened sanctuary pillar. Cracks are pointed and the capitals are anchored.

Rooms are cleaned, benches restored, and much debris removed.

1896 At the Serra Church, iron tie-rods stabilize leaning adobe walls. The church is re-roofed with Oregon pine and missing and broken roof tiles are replaced. The corridor is roofed with pine rafters, redwood sheeting and asphaltum for waterproofing.

1902 – 1903
The Landmarks Club continues repair work at San Juan Capistrano:

The comedor (dining room) roof is replaced and the chimney repaired.

The cuartel (soldiers' barracks) is re-roofed with timbers and shingles.

Four hundred tons of debris is removed.

An irrigation system is provided.

1906 At the Great Stone Church, the Landmarks Club does repair work on the walls and dome of the sacristy.

1910 Father St. John O'Sullivan arrives and takes up residence at the Mission. His interest and enthusiasm earn him the title, "Restorer of the Mission."

1912 Serra Church: The Landmarks Club obtains some 3,000 roof tiles and replaces the disintegrating ones on the church.

1914 Serra Statue: At the direction of Father O'Sullivan, John Van Rensselaer creates a Serra Monument and has it placed at the Mission entrance.

1915 Heavy rains cause much damage to the Old Mission: An adobe wall on the west end of the south wing gives way; one of the corridor arches collapses; the Great Stone Church sacristy leaks badly and the main pillars of the church show signs of disintegrating. The main dome over the sanctuary is in danger of falling. A large portion of the west wall of the soldiers' barracks falls out.

The upper floor priest quarters in the south wing is remodeled.

1916 Heavy rains continue destruction at the Old Mission. The Landmarks Club comes to the rescue:
The kitchen wall is repaired from the core out.

A Fresno Scraper grades areas in order to drain water away from adobe walls.

At the Great Stone Church major work is done to repair and strengthen both the sacristy and the sanctuary domes. Steel rods are put in place to provide support for sagging walls. While the church is propped up with railway bridge timbers, the two main support pillars are disassembled, a steel core is put in place, new foundations poured, and the pillars reassembled stone by stone.

The west wall of the cuartel (soldiers' barracks) is rebuilt.

1916 A gatehouse is built and, for the first time, an Admission Fee is charged for visitors in order to help with the expenses of maintenance and preservation.

1917 The cuartel (soldiers' barracks): Its walls are repaired and mission tiles replace the shingle roof. The land is graded to drain water away from the building.

The comedor (dining room) is again repaired.

The old sacristy built in the corner of the corridor of the south wing and the sala (reception room) is removed to restore the corridor to its original appearance.

An adobe wall is built to enclose the Mission and an elaborate front gate provides a visitors entrance.

Electric lights are installed at the Mission.

1918 The property west of the Mission (the railroad side) is sold to provide money for preservation work.

1919 A Gate House is built at the front entrance.

At the Great Stone Church: The sacristy is remodeled and put to use.

The Sacred Garden: A wall and gateway, enclosing the garden, is built between the Sala and the Great Stone Church. The lower half of the campanario (bell wall) is repaired and restored on the garden side.

1920 A fountain is built in the Sacred Garden.

The Serra Church: Major work begins on the plan to restore the Serra Church for use again as the Mission's church. (The Sala had been serving as the church since 1891.) The east wall of the Serra Church is faced with brick and strengthened with buttresses.

1922 The Serra Church is restored to its original length by rebuilding the old sanctuary north of the building. (It had been abandoned and left to ruin in Father Mut's time when its roof collapsed and a new wall was built up to meet the part of the roof that was still intact.) The graves of the padres are once again inside the church.

The gold retablo (altar wall) arrives from Los Angeles and is placed in storage while awaiting assembly in the restored church.

1923 New floor tiles are set in the Serra Church.

1924 Interior work is completed on the Serra Church.

In November 2nd, Bishop John J. Cantwell presides at the re-dedication of the Serra Church

The fountain is built near the Mission entrance.

1927 – 1928
The north wing of the quadrangle is rebuilt and serves as a school, convent, and rectory.

1930 The large Fountain of the Four Evangelists is built in the Mission's inner patio.

1933 Monsignor St. John O'Sullivan passes away. Father Arthur Hutchinson becomes the Mission's pastor.

1934 The gardens and walkways are laid out in the quadrangle patio.

1935 – 1936
Excavations made along the west side of the west wing reveal the remains of tallow vats, soap works, facilities for tanning hides, and the original irrigation system.

1940 – 1941
Long, plaster lined vats – possibly for soaking hides – are unearthed on the west side of the west wing.

1951 Father Arthur Hutchinson passes away. Monsignor Vincent Lloyd-Russell becomes the Mission's pastor.

1952 The east wing, north of the Serra Church, is restored to its original length.
This portion, which completes the quadrangle on that side becomes a new, two story rectory.

The Mission's hall/gymnasium is built just north of the Old Mission.

1954 – 1955
An eight-classroom addition is built north of the 1928 elementary school.

1970 – 1975
The ruins of the west wing are removed and the whole wing is rebuilt. This encloses the quadrangle as in the old mission times.

1976 The Mission celebrates its Bicentennial.

1976 Monsignor Vincent Lloyd Russell passes away. Father Paul M. Martin succeeds him.

1982 – 1986
A modern church is built for the Mission on the north side at the corner of Camino Capistrano and Acjachema. It is a replica of the Great Stone Church, but proportionately larger to accommodate the larger population.

1987 Cardinal Timothy Manning presides at the dedication of the new church.

1990 – 2003
The Mission undergoes major repairs in order to meet earthquake stabilization requirements

The Great Stone Church undergoes extensive work in a major preservation effort.

2000 Pope John Paul II honors the San Juan Capistrano Church and declares it a Minor Basilica.

1999 – 2000
A larger, modern school is constructed and replaces the 1955 structure.

2002 – 2003
A Pastoral Center is constructed as a center housing the parish's principal offices and meeting rooms.

2003 The United States Conference of Bishops designates Mission San Juan Capistrano as a National Shrine.

On July 1, the Very Reverend Arthur J. Holquin, S.T.L., becomes pastor following the resignation of Monsignor Paul Martin.

2005 Work begins on the Grand Retablo for the Mission Basilica.

2007 Cardinal William Levada, Prefect for the Congregation for the Doctrine of the Faith, blesses the Basilica's altar and retablo.

2008 Extensive work is completed on the refurbishing of the Serra Church.

Determination and Hard Work

Whenever there is a new day, there are new things to do. New leadership at the Mission has taken up the task of preservation and restoration with zeal to equal or excel the important work of their predecessors. Under the direction of the Pastor, Monsignor Arthur A. Holquin, S.T.L., and the Mission's Executive Administrator, Mechelle Lawrence-Adams, many important accomplishments have taken place. I am happy to have her relate these successes:

"In 2003, the Mission Preservation Foundation began an exciting chapter in the preservation of Mission

San Juan Capistrano. This was set in motion with the development and adoption of a Five Year Strategic Plan outlining the preservation priorities for the following years.

"The first step toward measurable and significant accomplishment was to ensure that the Great Stone Church stabilization project was completed as quickly as possible. Not only was it necessary to complete the exterior conservation treatment of the structure, and ensure seismic integrity, the project also included the need to install:

-A highly durable, collapsible, and visually appropriate railing for security purposes to separate the altar area from pedestrian traffic.

-A protective textile and decomposed granite covering over the highly sensitive and historic diamond shaped tile flooring.

-Marble coverings and interpretive outlines over the crypt in the sanctuary area.

-An interpretive display to house two of the original bells cast for the mission, in the original footprint of the bell tower that was once part of the church.

"In the summer of 2004, the Foundation shifted its attention from the Great Stone Church to the preservation of the Serra Chapel. That effort began with a conditions assessment to determine the needs and budget associated with the potential project. The building had fallen into significant disrepair. It needed more than maintenance. It needed careful, skillful conservation work carried out according to the standards of the National Trust for the Care and Treatment of Historic Buildings. The first cost estimate was $1 million, but the ultimate cost came in at just under $1.8 million. Nevertheless, it ensured the longevity of the Chapel for future generations.

"There were many tasks associated with the Serra Chapel Conservation Project. The staff began with the first ever fumigation and termite treatment of the site using thirty-six tents over a four-day period. Following this, the team worked on:

-Repairing the interior of the St. Peregrine Chapel (including replacing lost portions of roofing and stabilizing severely deteriorated wood rafter tails, repairing failing adobe, and applying a new coat of plaster).

-Retaining the services of John Griswold, a highly respected conservator, to determine the extent of the remaining original gilding on the 400-years-old Golden Retablo. Mr. Griswold and his staff discovered that most of the original gilding remained in tact under layers of improperly applied paint and poorly applied gilding. The twelve-month conservation project to remove the paint was completed in 2007.

-Retaining the services of Aneta Zebala, Paintings Conservation, to repair and conserve the historic Stations of the Cross collection. Each of the paintings was placed in new hand carved frames. gilded and painted in the Spanish Colonial style by Marisa Kumziga.

-May Paintings Conservators tended to the old decorations that embellished the entrance way to the Serra Chapel. Their team stabilized cracks, replaced lost plaster, and painted areas where finishes were lost or worn away. They repeated this process throughout the highly decorated nave and sacristy. It took nearly a year to complete this delicate work.

-Patrick Edwards of Antique Refinishers took on the work of conserving and restoring the chapel's thirty-eight pews and kneelers that dated to the 1920s.

-Marisa Kumziga conserved two of the gilded wooden candlesticks adorning the retablo. She cleaned, stabilized and repaired them, thus allowing previously improperly applied paint to be removed.

"Other areas of the mission also received needed attention. This included community outreach, education program development, security systems, preventative maintenance, event management, and more.

"In keeping with the Foundations focus on preservation, it was determined that new efforts center on the museum development and artifact management. A generous donor made possible the hiring of a full-time museum conservator who would inventory and photo document every mission artifact. This evolved to include thoughtful policies regarding collection storage and conservation.

"During this time, the historic statue of Our Lady of Pilar was restored its rightful place in the Serra Chapel.

"Patrick Edwards fabricated complimentary and appropriate furnishings for the St. Peregrine Chapel. Kneelers and furnishings were built to scale to better accommodate that small space.

" A very serious problem was discovered at the East door and supporting wall surface of the Serra Chapel. Due to significant deterioration, the main support header and the surrounding wall area threatened to collapse. A grant from the California Mission Foundation made possible the emergency repairs.

"A museum quality lighting designer developed a plan for lighting the interior of the Serra Chapel. The new system allowed for better lighting in an environmentally friendly and more efficient manner with careful thought given to prevent any negative effect on the Chapel's decorations and other artwork.

"While all this occurred, additional much needed and important site work was carried out that included preserving the 18th century South Wing building, conserving the walls and wall finishes comprising the Sacred Garden, and cleaning and conserving the world famous historic bell wall or campanario. Critically important conservation was completed on the interior finishes in the South Wing's padre's quarters with one room now revealing an earlier decorative scheme after layers of inappropriate paint had been removed. Throughout the site, the small preservation Team also worked to re-point failing bricks, crumbling adobe, and compromised arches in the corridors throughout the Mission.

"Staff also installed temperature and environmental monitoring systems to determine humidity and temperature levels in the museum wing since the environment greatly accelerates or hastens the rate of artifact deterioration. The preservation team also measured lighting levels in the Portola and Native American rooms and determined that all of the exhibits were over illuminated and above the recommended museum levels.

"In the ensuing years the Mission continued its focus on conservation of the Serra Chapel. Investment to upgrade the site (using donated gifts and funds, and available operating revenues) was a top priority. Progress was made in many areas: completing the Serra Chapel, carrying out the repairs of the arcade roofing,, installation of the fire safety system, installation of new museum quality lighting and chandeliers, and the final completion of the conservation of the Stations of the Cross paintings.

"Meanwhile, the Central Courtyard walkway received a much-needed treatment with the import of over 210 tons of fill material to allow the installation of decomposed granite over failed, uneven, and difficult cobblestone walkways. (A test case for making this improvement had been experimented with at the Great Stone Church where it was also difficult to navigate a shorter walkway). The goal of providing an historically compatible appearance and improving the area for both young and elderly visitors was quickly realized in one of the most stunning views of the Mission. The public's response was appreciative and enthusiastic.

"Concurrently over the next several years, staffing levels in the Facilities Department gradually increased as the organization came to better identify the immediate and future work needed to protect and enhance the Mission. During the past fiscal period the Facilities Department upgraded the restrooms, improved the front gate admissions ticket office, installed new signs throughout the grounds, removed broken and non-working lighting systems, deep cleaned the site, expanded security coverage, and developed greater maintenance coverage.

"By early 2008 the Serra Chapel project began to wind down with the installation of new roofing over covered corridors, the installation of security and fire safety systems, plans for the conservation treatment of two of the silver processional pieces found in the Serra Chapel, and the preparation of a new cross to accompany the Serra Statue in the front courtyard (c. 1915).

"Completed on time and under budget, some funds remained available to conserve other significant elements previously not included as part of the project, including the conservation of at least two historically significant paintings.

"A list of accomplishments over a five year period is impressive and exciting, and yet there remains so much more to be done. Mission San Juan Capistrano continues to make new history while being a vestige of the past and providing important contemporary resources for the community and individuals of all ages."

Mechelle Lawrence-Adams, May, 2009

San Juan Mission Capistrano June 4th/95

› 1917

2939 Mission San Juan Capistrano, Cal., founded 1776, ruins of the cloisters.
Photo, San Francisco.

Ruins of Old Mission at San Juan Capistrano, Founded in 1776 W.H.F. 324

APRIL, 1901. Vol. XIV, No. 4

A DESERT JOURNEY
SOME NATIVE BULBS
EARLY CALIFORNIA

Richly Illustrated

"LOS PAISES DEL SOL DILATAN EL ALMA"

THE LAND OF SUNSHINE

THE MAGAZINE OF

CALIFORNIA AND THE WEST

EDITED BY CHAS. F. LUMMIS

AT SAN JUAN CAPISTRANO MISSION.

10 CENTS A COPY

LAND OF SUNSHINE PUBLISHING CO., Incorporated
121½ South Broadway, Los Angeles.

$1 A YEAR

Father St. John O'Sullivan and Charles F. Lummis

North corridor

Soldiers' barracks 1917

Serra Chapel restoration in 1920

Great stone church in 1916

North wing restoration

Old "Acu"

Corridor

Entrance gate

Fountain of the Four Evangelists in 1930

Transformation of the inner courtyard

MISSION PAGEANT

by Garnet Holme

of

SAN JUAN

CAPISTRANO

every SATURDAY and SUNDAY at 230

during OCTOBER 1924

WITHIN THE MISSION WALLS!

Legend of the Swallows

The Legend of the Swallows is a remarkable story, a gem of California Romance that has captured the imaginations and delighted the hearts of millions. It is a treasure of poetic simplicity, a pretty blend of nature and faith evoking the spirit of Saint Francis who discerned the Divine in even the most humble of creation.

As it is told, the swallows seem to honor Saint Joseph – patron of all the California missions. They flock to Mission San Juan Capistrano on his feast day, March 19th. There they make their homes and produce a new generation. Then, after their sojourn in the California sun, they depart on October 23rd with the blessing of San Juan Capistrano whose feast day it is. They fly away just as mysteriously and faithfully as when they arrived. This curious cycle has repeated itself at the Mission for as long as anyone could remember – perhaps, centuries.

Although mention of the swallows at Capistrano first appeared in the Overland Monthly in 1915, it was Father St. John O'Sullivan who launched the legend in 1930. He wrote about it in a series of stories that he had collected from elders of Capistrano. Together with Charles Francis Saunders, a professional writer, he had some of these stories published in a book entitled *Capistrano Nights*. In the last chapter, he wrote about the swallows. He recalled watching a local merchant knocking down the swallows' nests that had accumulated under the eves of his establishment. To the merchant, they were a blight, an eyesore, and a dirty nuisance. To the soft and sentimental heart of Father O'Sullivan, their destruction seemed something of a crime against the innocent, demolishing the swallows' hard work and leaving them homeless. In his book, he tells his reaction as he watched them scatter: "Come on, swallows. I'll give you shelter, Come to the Mission. There's room enough for all." He then repeats the local lore about the pious and punctual return of the swallows on Saint Joseph's Day. Little did he know how this "Legend of the Swallows" would be picked up and find a re-telling far beyond the readers of *Capistrano Nights*.

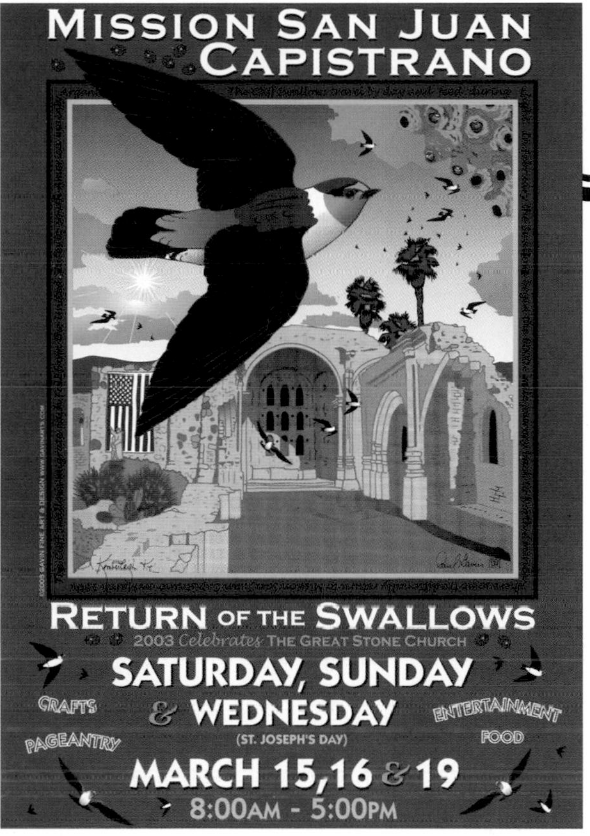

Gavin Fine Art and Design

The science of the swallow, the petrochelidon pyrrhonota, is certainly not as much fun as the story. Ornithologists describe the cliff swallow as a small bird – about the size of a common sparrow – that migrates annually between Argentina and California, a distance of about 6,000 miles. In the fall in South America they depart for California where it is springtime. Their journey lasts about a month. They fly about fifteen hours a day and about eighteen miles an hour. Taking advantage of favorable air currents, they fly at an altitude between 2,000 and 6,000 feet, thus avoiding most airborne predators. Around mid-March they arrive in the agricultural valleys of California. In spite of their long flight, they have little time to rest. They build their gourd-like nests of mud and grass and line the interior with soft feathers. In this "adobe hacienda" the mating pairs produce three or four eggs – two broods a year. The incubation period lasts only two weeks. The newly hatched have little beaks that must be fed. The search for food produces a busy, noisy frenzy of activity. The swallows have amazing speed and the ability to sharply change directions. This enables them to capture their food – insects – even in flight. After a long summer of feasting on this diet, they instinctively know it is time for a change. In the fall, about October, they abandon their California homes and depart for Argentina where springtime is beginning to blossom. This cycle repeats itself year after year and never ceases to amaze all who observe the process. If not a miracle, it is certainly a great wonder of nature.

Father O'Sullivan died in 1933, so he really didn't get to see in his lifetime what would happen to his story. Ed Ainsworth, an editor for the Los Angeles Times, was intrigued by it and every March 19th he would write about it in the paper. In 1936, a popular radio reporter broadcast the "Return of the Swallows" on live national radio. In the presence of a large crowd that included California Governor Frank Merriman, he dramatically announced to his anxiously awaiting listeners that the "Skies were blackened with swallows." It may have been an exaggeration, but it was interesting. From that time on, the little swallows and the small mission town of San Juan Capistrano became famous in the major cities of the nation and beyond.

In 1939, composer Leon Rene wrote his song, "When the Swallows Come Back to Capistrano." It was a big hit and sold over three million records. Glenn Miller, Gene Autry, the Ink Spots, and other popular music artists recorded it. Capistrano swallows became celebrities and now it was the visitors who flocked to the Old Mission to see for themselves what it was all about.

In 1940, John Steven McGroarty, California's poet laureate, made this observation in his column for the Los Angeles Times:

"The Mystical return on St. Joseph's Day each year of the swallows to the old Mission of San Juan Capistrano is well known throughout the world. The watching skies are full of the swallows' wings when the annual event roles around. With their bright wings flashing in the morning sun the swallows have never failed through a century and more of time to seek again their well-loved nests."

Certainly, conditions were ideal at Capistrano for the swallows to make their summer home among the ruins of the Old Mission. The climate was right. The building materials for their nests were at hand. And, especially along the Trabuco and San Juan Creeks, there were plenty of insects. No one minded if the arrival of the swallows meant the disappearance, or at least the lessening of mosquitoes.

Lately, the celebrated swallows, like Hollywood celebrities, have sought to preserve their privacy and seek secure refuge away from the well meaning, but over enthusiastic public. By the 1970s it was becoming obvious to disappointed visitors to the Mission that the swallows were not returning in numbers as in previous times. Each year it seemed less and less. What was happening?

Various reasons for the flight of the swallows from the Mission have been offered. It has been noted that the swallows' return seemed to diminish in proportion to Capistrano's growth in population and development. Some suggested that the creeks were dry much of the year and made the area less inviting. Furthermore, improved and effective pesticides lessened the insect population, vital to the swallows' diet.

Be this as it may, the swallows still do come to Capistrano, just "not so much" to the Mission. They now favor nesting under freeway overpasses, bridges, and outlying buildings in rural, less busy locations.

Efforts to get the swallows to return to the Mission have been as comic as they have been unsuccessful. Carefully prepared mud patches, artificial ceramic nests, commercially released lady bugs, and recordings of swallow mating calls have all failed to entice any except the occasional odd swallow that darts by to see what the humans are up to now.

Mission San Juan Capistrano and in fact the whole Capistrano community owes gratitude to these international fliers. The unexpected popularity of the "Legend of the Swallows" brought an increase of visitors and an entirely welcome increase in income to the Mission. This unexpected support was something of a "miracle" to those who wondered how in heaven's name the Old Mission could survive. The preservation and restoration of this historic treasure is due, in no small measure, to the little birds with the big name, petrochelidon pyrrhonota.

Good morning, Mr. Swallow
come from far away.
We are glad to see you on Saint Joseph's Day.
Flitting in the sunshine, we can see you all
Building up your houses
on the Mission wall.
(Mission Children's Song)

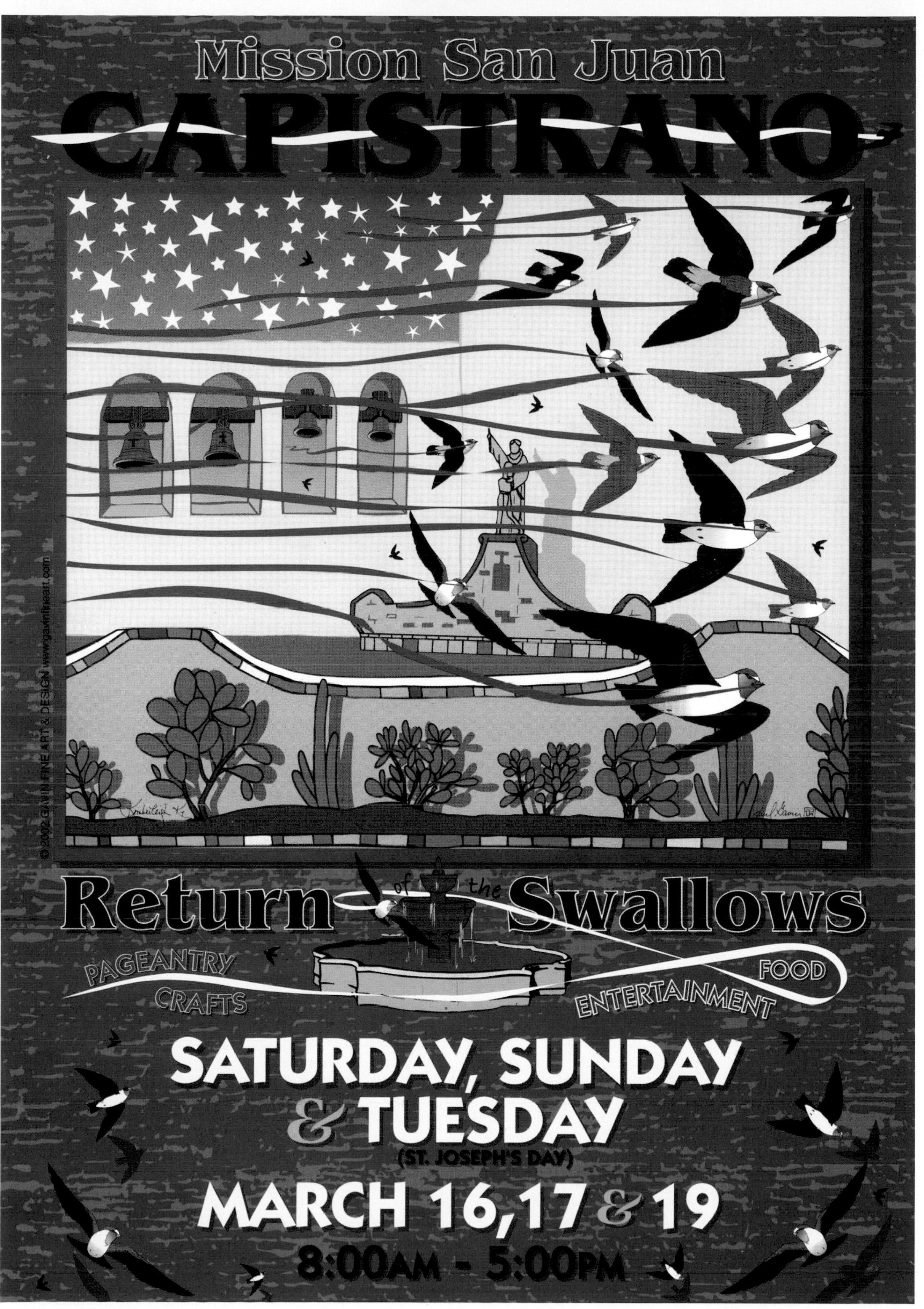

Gavin Fine art and design

EL ADOBE
DE CAPISTRANO

Las Golondrinas
Mexican Food

WELCOME TO
CAPISTRANO
Jewel of the Missions
HOME OF THE SWALLOWS
FREE SWALLOW STORY HERE

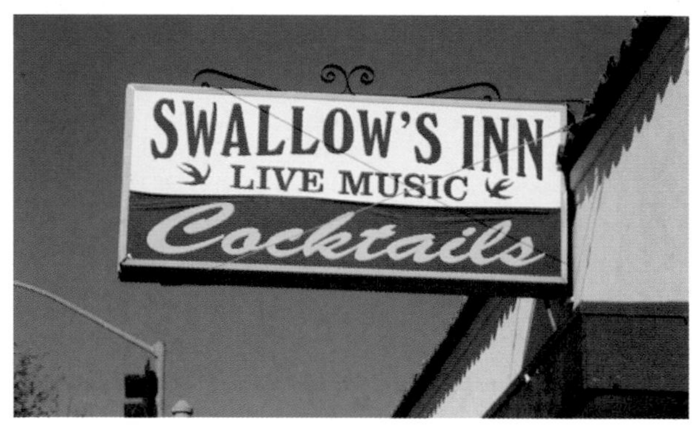
SWALLOW'S INN
LIVE MUSIC
Cocktails

L'Hirondelle

When the Swallows Come Back to Capistrano

Words and Music by LEON RENE'

Sole Selling Agent: **LEON RENE PUBLICATIONS**
2124 WEST 24TH STREET
LOS ANGELES, CALIFORNIA

LEON RENE' PUBLICATIONS

XII The Padres

Saint John of Capistrano

St. John of Capistrano was a highly respected lawyer, judge, and governor. He enjoyed much success in the secular world, but surpassed those achievements when he surrendered his talents to the service of Christ and His people.

John was born on June 24, 1386, in the Italian village of Capistrano in the Province of Abruzzi. His mother was Italian and his father French. She was a devout Catholic of the Amici family. His father, Anthony, was a French Baron who came across the Alps with the army of Louis I of Anjou. While John was still quite young, his father and brothers were killed during one of the many political struggles that plagued the region.

John's loving mother saw to it that he received a first class education. She supplied him with a tutor when he was six years old. When he was fifteen, she sent him to the University of Perugia where he excelled in both civil and church law. His exceptional competence and keen sense of judgement won him great respect and the promise of a very lucrative career. In 1412 he married the daughter of the count of San Valentino. That same year he became Governor of Perugia.

Caught up in a bitter political controversy, John's life took a sharp turn in direction. His enemies cast him into prison. It was during this time of unsolicited solitude that he experienced a deep religious calling. Following his release, he abandoned the pursuit of worldy power, gave himself over to Christ, and became an humble Franciscan. It is not clear what happened to his wife; perhaps, she passed away. Anyway, he became a professed Franciscan on October 5, 1416. He was thirty-one years old.

Following religious studies, he entered the priesthood on November 14, 1418. Afterwards, he worked with the saintly Bernardine of Siena. This privileged collaboration helped to deepen and shape his spiritual quest. When Pope Nichols V canonized Saint Bernardine of Siena in 1450, Fray John of Capistrano was present for the ceremonies.

John's calling to the life of a humble Franciscan did not lead to a life of humble obscurity. His profound eloquence made him a famous and much sought after preacher, not only on the Italian Peninsula, but in other countries of central Europe. His considerable spiritual and intellectual skills led to a leadership position with his Order and special missions delegated by the Holy See. When the superior forces of invading Muslim Turks threatened Christian Europe, Fray John was assigned to preach and organize a defensive crusade. Together with the great military commander, John Hunyadi, he led the troops in the defeat of the enemy at the Battle of Belgrade in 1456. Like Hunyadi, he did not live long to savor the victory. Fray John of Capistrano passed away on October 23, 1456. This day is observed in the Church as his feast day.

In spite of his worldly renown, St. John of Capistrano lived a life of exceptional austerity and exemplary religious commitment. His sincerity and zeal were unquestionable and his holiness was obvious. This remarkable Franciscan was beatified in 1690 and canonized by Pope Benedict XIII in 1724. The future Apostle of the Californias, Fray Junipero Serra, was eleven years old at the time.

Fr. Junipero Serra at San Juan Capistrano

As President of the California Missions, Father Junipero Serra exercised authority over Mission San Juan Capistrano from its first founding in 1775 until his death on August 28, 1784. When he first saw the place, it was not yet a mission. It was just a place near the El Camino Real, the rough road that led from his own mission, San Carlos at Carmel, to San Diego in the south. It was 1772 and he and Commander Pedro Fages with some troops were on their way there. It was his first overland trip through California. At this time, Carmel and Monterey were desperate for the supplies that had finally arrived at San Diego in August on board the ship San Antonio. This ship, under command of Captain Juan Pérez, had tried to reach Monterey but was turned back by contrary winds. The Captain decided to leave the supplies for the north at San Diego where they could be sent overland by pack train. When Father Serra and Commander Fages learned of this, they decided to head south to San Diego and see if they could persuade the Captain to try again. Otherwise, putting together a long mule train and traveling all the way to Monterey would be really difficult and require a very long time. On their way down, Father Serra, the Commander, and the soldiers arrived at San Gabriel on September 11th. They left there on the 13th and arrived at San Diego on the 16th. Since the Capistrano site is about midway between San Gabriel and San Diego, they must have seen the future site of San Juan Capistrano on September 14th or 15th. At San Diego they pleaded with Captain Pérez to reconsider his decision and bring the supplies up to Monterey. After some justifiable hesitation, he finally consented and made the trip successfully.

Father Serra stayed at San Diego for over a month. He felt frustrated in what he saw as Commander Fages's lack of cooperation in promoting the missions. On October 20, 1772, he sailed for Mexico on the San Carlos with the intention of meeting with his religious superiors and the viceroy in order to straighten out the problems in Alta California.

Father Serra's second visit to the Capistrano area was on his return from Mexico. He arrived at San Diego Bay aboard the Santiago on March 20, 1774. On April 6th, he began his overland trip to Monterey. He must have passed through the Capistrano area on about April 9th. The experience was not a pleasant one. Heavy rains and mud caused the trip to San Gabriel to last a full six days.

On Father Serra's third trip to the Capistrano area he actually stayed about a month to found the mission. At Serra's direction, Father Lasuén had attempted to found it in October of 1775. That failed because of the Indian uprising at San Diego. Serra was anxious to go down to San Diego, but was unable to to make the journey for seven months. Finally, he took passage on the San Antonio, which was heading down the coast from Monterey. He arrived at San Diego on July 11, 1776. Permission from the Viceroy to restore Mission San Diego and re-found Mission San Juan Capistrano arrived at San Diego on September 28. On October 25, with Fr. Gregorio Amurrió, eleven soldiers, and a mule train bearing supplies, he set out for the Capistrano site. They arrived there about October 30 or 31. On November 1, 1776, All Saints Day, he formally founded Mission San Juan Capistrano. While the place was being readied he went to San Gabriel where he obtained cattle and supplies for the new mission. He remained at Capistrano until the end of November when he continued his trip north passing through the other missions on his way back to San Carlos. He had been at the new mission for about a month.

Normally, a bishop is the minister of the Sacrament of Confirmation. Since California was distant missionary territory, Father Serra, as President of the Alta California Missions, requested permission from Rome to administer this sacrament. Pope Clement XIV granted this privilege in 1774 as a ten-year permit. When Father Serra finally received notice of this in June of 1778, four years had already elapsed. Anxious to avoid any further delay, he left Carmel on August 24 taking passage on the Santiago, He finally arrived at San Diego Bay on September 15. He stayed there over a month, confirming during this period 610 people. He left San Diego on October 19th and reached San Juan Capistrano – sixty-nine miles distant – in the afternoon of October 22nd.

Because of a shortage of water, the Mission had been relocated to its current site that same month on October 4th. This was Serra's fourth visit to Capistrano and his first visit to the new location. A small church had already been prepared and it was in this new church that the Father Presidente celebrated Mass, baptized, and confirmed. He provided this account in his personal Confirmation Book:

"On October 23, 1778, the feast of the most glorious San Juan Capistrano, in the new Mission of the same San Juan Capistrano de Quanis-savit, which I had reached on the eve of the feast, after the High Mass which I sang solemnly, the sermon on the holy Patron and on the holy Sacrament of Confirmation, and after reading in the vernacular the faculty to confer it, granted by the Holy See, with the assistance of the two Missionary Fathers of said Mission, the Father Lector Pablo de Mugártegui and Father Gregório Amurrió, retaining the same sacerdotal vestments, I confirmed in due form the fifty-seven neophytes who were disposed and prepared for that important function. On the Sunday immediately following, the 25th of said month and year, in the same manner I confirmed sixteen. On the feast of the holy Apostles Saint Simon and Saint Jude Thaddeus, I confirmed three; and on the eighth day of the holy Patron I confirmed the last, who were eight. Of all who had thus far been baptized, two were missed and they could not be found. Therefore the confirmed were 147, whose entries with the names, circumstances, and the sponsors are noted in the special book, which for said purposes was commenced and arranged in due form, and to which I refer. The adults I instructed and disposed very much to my delight, on account of the skill that I observed in those interpreters and the affection of those who listened. The godfathers and godmothers, after giving the benediction to their godchildren on all the days mentioned, I reminded of their obligation. On the day of the last Confirmations, in the afternoon, I started on the road to the next mission with the consolation of leaving that new foundation, which on the third day after my departure had not completed the second year of its existence, in such a promising state spiritually and temporally. I witness whereof I signed this – Father Junipero Serra."

The Mission Book of Baptisms also shows that on October 22 and 24, 1778, he baptized twenty-six young boys and girls from seven different Capistrano villages. He made the entries in the book himself.

Father Serra decided to stay on for the Mission's second anniversary, November 1st, All Saints Day. He celebrated Mass that morning and left that afternoon for the next mission, San Gabriel.

On Serra's return to Carmel, Governor Felipe de Neve challenged his permit to administer Confirmations. At that time there was an arrangement between Spain and the Holy See. For the support and protection of the Catholic Church in Spain and its colonies, the King and his representatives had the right to review and decide on various Church appointments and decrees. This was called the royal patronage, the "patronato real."

The papal document permitting Father Serra to administer Confirmation indeed had the royal pase of the King's Council of the Indies and his Viceroy in Mexico City.

However, the original document was retained at the Missionary College of San Fernando in Mexico City. Serra's superior simply informed him of the permit and sent him various Roman documents pertinent to the administration of the sacrament. Obviously, neither he nor Serra expected the governor to interfere. Nevertheless, Neve protested. He insisted on examining the original document and claimed the necessity of adding on his own pase as vice patron of the province. Serra considered this just another harassment from a governor he already considered an impediment to his missionary goals. Both parties appealed to their superiors. This sent the issue into a protracted bureaucratic process hampered by inevitable slow communications. This effectively prevented Father Serra from exercising his faculty to confirm until August 16, 1781, when his right to confirm was verified by all the authorities. The governor lost the challenge, but Serra lost the time. He was not getting any younger and his permit was due to run out in July of 1784.

In March of 1782, Father Serra traveled overland down to San Gabriel, confirming at the missions along the way. From there he proceeded to the coastal channel where he founded the long postponed Mission of San Buenaventura. He also went to Santa Barbara where he thought he was going to found that mission, but Governor Neve would only permit the founding of the Santa Barbara Presidio. Disappointed, Serra returned home to San Carlos at Carmel. By this time he was nearly worn out. Age and infirmity had taken their toll. His chronic leg ailment had become worse and sharp pains in his chest further aggravated his condition. He began to sense his end was approaching.

In spite of this, Father Serra was determined, if it was God's will, to visit all the missions again, administer Confirmations, and bid a prayerful farewell to all his fellow missionaries. He took passage on the La Favorita and arrived at San Diego on September 6, 1783.

Father Serra spent a full month at Mission San Diego. He baptized an Indian child there and, over a period of eight days, confirmed 233 persons. He then headed north, setting out from San Diego on October 7th. Father Fermin Lasuén , concerned about the Father President, accompanied him as far as San Juan Capistrano. They arrived there on October 9th.

This was Father Serra's fifth and last visit to Capistrano. It had already been five years since he administered Confirmations there in 1778. Then the Mission had just been relocated and had only the priests' quarters, a very small chapel, and the most basic necessities. Father Pablo Mugártegui and Father Gregorio Amúrrio had been its missionaries. Father Mugártegui was still there, but Father Vicente Fuster had replaced Father Amurrió who had returned to Mexico in 1779. Now the mission had expanded living quarters, a kitchen, warehouses, storerooms, workshops, corrals, and a garden. The new church in which he would confirm is the church that still remains and is now called the "Serra Chapel." The north wing had not yet been built and there were no tiled roofs or corridors, but the basic shape of the Mission was already in place. The Mission Indian population was already close to four hundred. The livestock and agricultural products were doing well. Serra who founded the Mission must have been happy to see the progress.

On October 12, 1783, the Feast of Our Lady of the Pillar (Pilár de Saragoza) he confirmed ninety children with the assistance of Fathers Mugártegui and Fuster. On October 13th, the Feast of the Relics of St. Daniel, he confirmed 123 persons. On the 14th he administered the sacrament to seven more and, on October 15th, just one more. In all, he confirmed 221 at San Juan Capistrano. He had been at the Mission for just over a week. In his Confirmation Book he wrote: "I set out from that Mission with the affectionate embraces of the Fathers on said 15th day of October, 1783." He was not to see them again in this life. Although, with difficulty, he completed his confirmation tour, he was nearly spent. He passed away at San Carlos in Carmel on August 28, 1784.

del mismo San Diego, al fin de mi Missa, q. fue la mayor, con asistª. d todo el
Pueblo, hecha mi Platica Doctrinal, y Panegyrica del Stmo. Sacramto. con los ornamentos Sacerdotales del Sto. Sacrificio, y asistencia del R. P. Fr. Fermin Lasuen
sobredho, Confirme â treynta, y ocho, â saber, quatro neophitos d la Mision, y los
demas de la tropa, y vezinos de dho Real. — — — — 038. //
It. dia 30 immto. siguiente, buelto ya â dha Misn. confirme al fin de mi Missa
con asistª. d ambos PP. de dha Mision, y assi revestido â cinco neoph. .. 005. //
It. en 5. de Octubre, Domingo del Ssmo. Rosario de Maria Ss. en la Iglesia d dha
Mision, al fin de mi Missa cantada, Confirme â quinze neoph. -- 015. //
It. en 6. immto. siguiente despues d mi Missa &c. Confirme â uno — 001. //
Con las quales partidas, asciendió el numº. d Confirmaciones hechas, en esta
mi visita, en dho San Diego, â dos cientas treynta y tres. Los PP. Ministros dhs
quedaron con el encargo de escrivirlas con la devida distincion en el Libro
â ellas destinado, â continuacion d las q. celebre en la misma Mision en
el año de 1778 como se nota en la foja 3. de este libro, q. eran 610. Al fin de
cada uno de dhs sagrados Actos, di â los Confirmados solemnte. la Bendicion
segun la formula del Pontifical Romano, ê Instruccion d la Sag. Cong. De propa-
ganda Fide, y â los Padrinos, y Madrinas adverti el parentesco espiritual, y
oblign. q. contraxeron, y haviendome detenido en dha Mision un mes cabal
el 26 despues d aquella Christiandad al dia siguiente â la Sta. Confirmacion,
7. de dho mes, tome mi camino, aunq. con el dolor d quedar algunos d los mon-
tes sin Confirmar, pª la Mision sigte. y pª q. todo conste, lo firmé. =

Fr. Junipero Serra

Mision de San Juan Capistrano — Confirmaciones 221.

En 12 de Octubre, Domingo, y dia d N.ª Sra. Maria Sª. de la Columna,
ô del Pilar de Zaragoza, en la Iglesia de la Mission de Sn. Juan de Capistrano d Quanis-savit, â la q. tres dias antes llegue, haviendo cantado la Missa
mayor d aquel solemne dia, permaneciendo en el Altar, y con los Ornamentos
Sacerdotales, asistido d los RR. PP. Fr. Pablo de Mugartegui, y Fr. Vicente
Fuster Ministros d aquella Mision, hechas al Auditorio las advertencias
convenientes, administre el Sto. Sacramto. de la Confirmacion â los q. la soli-
citud d q. aquellos zelosos Ministros tuvo dispuestos, y me presentó para
aquel primer acto q. fueron noventa parvulos — — — 090. //
It. dia 13 immto. siguiente, dedicado â los SS. Mm. d N. Sag. Religⁿ. San Daniel,
y Compª. y dia d Indulgª., al fin de mi Missa, con los Ornamtos. d ella, y asistª.
de dhs PP. confirme mayor numº. pª aquel dia dispuesto, por los mismos
PP. y â mi presentado, q. fueron ciento veynte, y tres — — 123. //
It. dia 14 immto. tambien al fin de mi Missa, con los Ornamtos. Sacerdotales
de ella, y asistª. de dhs PP. Ministros, Confirme â siete — — 007. //
Y finalmte. en el dia 15. sigte. al fin d mi Missa, Confirme uno — 001. //
Con lo q. fueron los Confirmados, en esta Mision, en esta mi visita, dos-
cientos, veynte, y uno, y asegurandome los dhs PP. d q. no hallavan modo
de traher â algunos, q. faltavan â Confirmar, determine, pª el dia sigte. //
// 4076. //   // mi

Father Serra's record of confirmation at San Juan Capistrano

› *Father O'Sullivan's tribute to Father Junipero Serra in 1913*

JUNIPERO SERRA

Missionaries of San Juan Capistrano

Father Junípero Serra directed that two missionaries serve in each of the California Missions. This policy was intended to provide support and companionship in their labors as well as, at least, a minimal sense of religious community as Franciscan clergy. The following list of missionaries serving at San Juan Capistrano is set out according to the pairings assigned by the Father Presidente of the Missions. The age of the priest at the time of his arrival at Capistrano follows his name. The years shown is parenthesis indicates the years they served together. Each priest's native land is also shown.

The Spanish Period 1769 – 1821

Fray Junípero Serra, President of the Missions

Founder of Mission San Juan Capistrano	(1776)	Spain
Fray Pablo Mugártegui (40)	(1776 – 1779)	Spain
Fray Gregorio Amurrió (32)		Spain
Fray Pablo Mugártegui	(1779 – 1789)	Spain
Fray Vicente Fuster (37)		Spain
Fray Vicente Fuster	(1789 – 1800)	Spain
Fray Juan Norberto de Santiago (28)		Spain
Fray Juan Norberto de Santiago	(1800 – 1809)	Spain
Fray José Faura (27)		Spain
Fray Francisco Suñer (46)	(1810 – 1814)	Spain
Fray José Barona (47)		Spain
Fray José Barona	(1814 – 1826)	Spain
Fray Gerónimo Boscana (39)		Spain

The Mexican Period

1821 – 1848

Fray José Barona	(1826 – 1831)	Spain
Fray José María de Zalvidea (46)		Spain

Secularization Decree of 1833

Fray José María de Zalvidea	(1831 – 1842)	Spain

(He served alone since no one was available to assist him.)

The Diocese of the Two Californias 1840
Bishop García Diego y Moreno, O.F.M.

No Resident Priest	(1842)	
Fray Tomás Esténaga (53)	(1843 – 1846)	Spain
Fray Vicente Pasqual Oliva (66)	(1846 – 1848)	Spain

The American Period
1848 – Current

No Resident Priest	(1848 – 1850)	
Rev. José María Rosales	(1850 – 1853)	Mexico

(He is the first diocesan priest assigned to San Juan Capistrano.)

Rev. Pedro Bagaría	(1853 – 1856)	Spain
Rev. Jayme Vila (24)	(1856 – 1857)	Spain
Rev. J. Molinier (51)	(1857 – 1859)	France
Rev.Vicente Llover	(1859 – 1863)	Spain
Rev. Miguel Durán (32)	(1863 – 1866)	Spain
Rev. Joseph Mut (33)	(1866 – 1886)	Spain
Rev. Miguel Durán (55)	(1886 – 1889)	Spain
No Resident Priest	(1889 – 1909)	

(During this period parishes at San Gabriel, Anaheim, Santa Ana, San Luis Rey, and Los Angeles occasionally sent a priest to tend to the people of San Juan Capistrano.)

Rev. Alfred Quetú (46)	(1909 – 1914)	France
Rev. Msgr. St. John O'Sullivan (36)	(1914 – 1933)	Ireland
Rev. Arthur Hutchinson (57)	(1933 – 1951)	U.S.A.
Rev. Msgr. Vincent Lloyd Russell (47)	(1951 – 1976)	Ireland
Rev. Msgr. Paul Martin (46)	(1976 – 2003)	U.S.A.
Rev. Msgr. Arthur A. Holquin, S.T. L. (55)	(2003 – Current)	U.S.A.

California Mission Presidents

Fr. Junípero Serra (1769 – 1784)
Fr. Francisco Palóu (1784 – 1785)
Fr. Fermín Francisco de Lasuén (1785 – 1803)
Fr. Estevan Tapis (1803 – 1812)
Fr. José Señan (1812 – 1815)
Fr. Mariano Payeras (1815 – 1819)
Fr. José Señan (1819 – 1823)
Fr. Vicente Francisco Sarría (1823 – 1825)
Fr. Narciso Durán (1825 – 1827)
Fr. José Sanchez (1827 – 1831)
Fr. Narciso Durán (1831 – 1838)
Fr. José Jimeno (1838 – 1844)
Fr. Narciso Durán (1844 – 1846)

Blessed Junipero Sera, O.F.M. (1713-1784)

Acknowledgements

I would like to thank Bishop Tod D. Brown for allowing me to serve in a position where I would be able to produce this book on Mission San Juan Capistrano. I am also grateful to Monsignor Arthur Holquin, Pastor of the Old Mission, and Mechelle Lawrence Adams, the Mission's Executive Administrator, for their support of this project. Special thanks are due to Linda L. Hughes for the beautiful watercolor images used throughout the book, Sharon Jones for calligraphy, and Doug Catiller of True Image Studio for the professional photography. I appreciate the assistance of Catherine Hayes and Christine Shook for enabling that photography. Thanks also go to Jim and Nancy Hastings of The Enlarger for their much-needed technical assistance.

I am grateful for the use of much of the book's artwork to Jean Stern of the Irvine Museum, Janine Salzman, Gavin Fine Art and Design, Swallow Creek Productions, Melissa Latham Stevens of St. John's College in Santa Fe, and the Collection of Edward H. and Yvonne Boseker.

I also want to acknowledge appreciation for the use of historical photographs provided by Don Tryon of the Historical Society of San Juan Capistrano, the San Juan Capistrano Mission Archives, the Santa Barbara Mission Archives, and the Mansfield Library of the University of Montana at Missoula.

I thank the staff of Editions du Signe for their hospitality and also for their expertise in bringing together in such a professional way all the elements of this book.

A major debt of gratitude is due to the Family of Thomas J. Tracy for their support of Old Mission San Juan Capistrano and this publication.

Thank you to all who have in anyway helped me to provide you with this history and pictorial tour of our beloved Mission San Juan Capistrano.

Rev. William Krekelberg

Publisher:

Éditions du Signe

1, rue Alfred Kastler - Eckbolsheim

B.P. 94 – 67038 Strasbourg, Cedex 2, France

Tel: ++33 (0) 3 88 78 91 91

Fax: ++33 (0) 3 88 78 91 99

www.editionsdusigne.fr

email: info@editionsdusigne.fr

Publishing director: Christian Riehl

Director of publication: Joëlle Bernhard

Author: Reverend William F. KREKELBERG

Layout: Éditions du Signe - Anthony Kinné

Photoengraving : Éditions du Signe - 108206

ISBN 978-2-7468-2291-7

Printed in China